". . . Negatively enabling behavior is examined with compassion, an understanding of human frailty, and an emphasis on the strength that parents and families have within themselves . . . [includes] a helpful state-by-state survey of treatment programs and support groups."

Publisher's Weekly, March 24, 1989

". . . Drastically depicts the vital role parents must play . . . Will help all readers develop the much-needed courage to turn defeat into victory!"

> Dr. Benjamin L. Hooks
> Executive Director
> National Association for the Advancement
> of Colored People (NAACP)

"It was a pleasure to appear with you on the 'MacNeil/Lehrer News Hour,' and I was greatly impressed by your sincerity and your knowledge . . . I only wish there had been more time for conversation."

> Michael S. Dukakis
> Governor, Massachusetts

"As executive producer of America's foremost psychology talk show for the past seven years, dozens of 'How To' books cross my desk every day. Ms. Becnel's book is unique, however, in that it is intensely personal and shares with the reader sensitive and illuminating stories of how addiction has tragically changed lives."

> Richard E. Chavez
> Executive Producer, "Dr. Toni Grant Show"
> KFI Radio, Los Angeles

"I am sure *Parents Who Help Their Children Overcome Drugs* will be helpful to the Subcommittee during any consideration of legislation dealing with the drug problem."

> Augustus F. Hawkins, Chairman of the
> Subcommittee on Elementary, Secondary, and
> Vocational Education

"Your interest in demand-side ideas for policy and program improvements in a national drug policy is consistent with mine and others' efforts in this area."

Pete Stark
Member of Congress, House of Representatives

"Much money is spent every year by the California Department of Rehabilitation to help youth who have a history of drug abuse become productive and economically self-sufficient citizens. If mothers and fathers in this state read *Parents Who Help Their Children Overcome Drugs*, our workload at the Department of Rehabilitation could be lowered by the number of young people who may no longer need our services. We are excited by this book because of the hope it promises."

Melinda Wilson, Assistant Deputy Director
Los Angeles Region, State of California
Department of Rehabilitation

"The majority of inmates at the Sybil Brand Institute for Women have abused drugs or alcohol and have been involved in drug-related crimes. Many of these women are young mothers themselves who are caught in a difficult-to-break pattern of criminality and substance abuse. *Parents Who Help Their Children Overcome Drugs* could help these women and eventually their children break the debilitating cycle."

Sybil Brand
Chairperson, County of Los Angeles
Institutional Inspections Commission

PARENTS

WHO HELP THEIR

CHILDREN

OVERCOME

DRUGS

BARBARA COTTMAN BECNEL

CompCare® Publishers

Minneapolis, Minnesota

Becnel, Barbara Cottman
    Parents Who Help Their Children Overcome Drugs/Barbara Cottman
    Becnel.

Bibliography: p.
Includes index.
    ISBN 0-89638-218-4
        1. Children—United States—Drug use. 2. Drug abuse—United
        States—Prevention. 3. Parenting—United States.
        I. Title.
HV5824.C45B43 1990
649'.4—dc19   90-30297
                              CIP

First printing, hardcover © 1989 RGA Publishing Group, Inc.

Cover design by Nancy MacLean

Inquiries, orders, and catalog requests should be addressed to
CompCare Publishers
2415 Annapolis Lane
Minneapolis, Minnesota 55441
Call toll free 800-328-3330
(Minnesota residents 612/559-4800)

 5   4   3   2   1
94   93   92   91   90

This book is for my son and sister who have helped me learn how to forgive and, thus, love myself.

Contents

Acknowledgments

I am grateful for the consummate talent of my editor, Janice Gallagher, who has helped me look better on paper than I could ever have imagined. A thank-you is in order as well for Jack Artenstein, my publisher, who demonstrated faith by providing me with the opportunity to write this book. I am appreciative of the patience and understanding displayed by my "daytime" boss, Daniel J. Flaming, whenever I showed up for work a little bleary-eyed from having stayed up late to write the night before. I want to acknowledge my good fortune to have such a close friend as Paula Manning, who continues to encourage me every step of the way.

Last, I want to offer a special thanks to my parents. Each one played a role in shaping my character: My mother is responsible for the tenacity and confidence I needed to undertake the task of writing this book; my birth father's strong belief in the importance of helping most anyone in need led to my choosing this topic; and my stepfather's courage to deal with his own co-dependent behavior bolstered me during those difficult moments when researching this book unearthed more about my own problems than I believed, at first, I could bear.

Parents Who Help Their Children Overcome Drugs

To Parents Who Want to Help Their Children Overcome Drugs

I wrote this book in part because I wanted to help others and in part because I wanted to help myself. For years I had known of my younger sister's struggles with drugs, yet for years I had been unable to accept the fact that she was a substance abuser, that she really needed treatment, and that my reluctance to face the truth contributed in some significant ways to her addictive behavior.

The 10½-year difference in our ages had on many occasions put me in the position of acting as my sister's surrogate parent. I changed her diapers, warmed bottles and baby food, and slept without moving for hours with my infant sister cradled securely in my arms. When as a teenager she had difficulties getting along with our mother after our father's death and mother's remarriage, I even took on the responsibility of supporting her during some of her time as a college student. When she left the campus for holiday vacations, she stayed with me in Washington, D.C., not with our mother and stepfather in Los Angeles.

Given that history, one would think that at the very least I would have recognized that my sister was in some type of trouble when her college grades started to plummet inexplicably and when, years later, she was unable to pay her bills and could not provide plausible explanations of what had happened to her money. But I didn't recognize the signs because I opted to keep my head in the sand. In retrospect, I simply didn't want to know that she had been using drugs for a number of years, starting with marijuana at 14 or 15 and ending with crack cocaine while pregnant during her mid-twenties.

These days, my sister is on the road to recovery, and so am I. We have both learned some important lessons, including the fact that her addictive personality was only one side of the coin. The way I related to her problem of substance abuse reflected a pattern of behavior on my part that was equally unhealthy. I was a co-dependent person whose own pathology of controlling and rescuing was triggered by my sister's pathology of manipulating in order to avoid responsibility for her chemical addiction.

My sister and I have also learned to accept that we are human, that we are imperfect, and that it is possible to carve out a constructive life despite our flaws and, most important, despite our mistakes. Through my participation in this book I have spoken to parents, their substance-abusing children, and drug-abuse professionals from all over the United States, and virtually every person I met reinforced that same lesson.

I am a writer, a sister, and a surrogate parent of sorts who has traveled the road on which you are about to embark. What I can say to you is this: Though the environment faced by parents who help their children overcome drugs is rife with challenges, it is also rife with opportunities for recovery. So, take heart in the book's underlying theme: A healthy family need not be perfect, only committed and courageous enough to work toward change.

How to Use This Book

This book has been organized to help parents move themselves and their family members through a process of healing that comprises a number of phases. To that end, the six chapters in this book represent clearly delineated stages, from denial to eventual recovery. Each chapter begins with descriptions of my personal experiences as a sibling and surrogate parent trying to help my younger sister during her struggle with substance abuse. Each chapter ends with a case study of a family who has a similar story to tell. In between are straightforward and realistic explanations of what is required of families who want to help their children overcome drugs.

Chapter One, "Good Looks Are Deceiving," examines how easy it was for my family—and is for families in general—to engage in self-deception: While we clung to our pristine image, my sister was developing a heavy habit of using drugs. Chapter Two, "Co-dependency—On Being Addicted to the Addict," describes the role parents unwittingly play in "enabling" their child to use drugs when they make excuses or rescue their offspring from the harsh consequences associated with chemical addiction. Chapter Two also points out that this compulsion of some parents to go to extremes to "get things back to normal" constitutes a behavioral pattern as unhealthy as their child's substance abuse.

Chapters Three and Four—"Hanging Tough" and "Raising the Bottom, or Hanging Tough Phase II"—deal with the necessary lines parents must draw when their chemically addicted child repeatedly disregards the family's and society's rules. Chapter Five, "Treatment Options," presents the range of healing options available. The last chapter, "Letting Go," provides a more tolerant perspective of what constitutes success and recovery. There are also three appendixes: (A) a description of each state's policies concerning private health insurance coverage for services that help treat substance abusers, (B) a state-by-state list of treatment centers and support groups, and (C) a list of references and suggested readings.

The six case studies represent families with children, ages 14 to 22, who are either in the process of recovery or who have completed one or more treatment programs. These testifiers hail from cities throughout the United States, though most of the children have in common the fact that they spent time at Spring Creek Community, a therapeutic boarding school in Thompson Falls, Montana. The headmaster, Steven W. Cawdrey, was especially helpful in enlisting the cooperation of families whom he believed would willingly discuss the circumstances that led to their children's enrollment at his school.

Still, there were times when one or the other parent he referred refused to speak. There were instances when both parents wanted to share their experiences but the child did not want to talk about what had happened. A number of the parents and children had therapists or drug-abuse counselors who were willing to report on why they believed the families were in trouble. Of those parents, young people, and drug-abuse professionals who agreed to participate in the project, most requested their names be changed for anonymity. The stories they tell, though, are real, poignant, and frequently tough. You may cringe, cry, or chuckle at moments when you read the straight talk from these parents, their children, and the experts they asked for help.

With every case study, you will hear from the following family members in the order cited: mother, father, child in trouble, and sibling. I did very little editing and summarizing. For the most part, I transcribed the interviews and reported them as they were expressed to me. Given the way I decided to handle the material, there are inconsistencies, at times. For example, a father's depiction of a particular incident may not jibe with his daughter's version of what happened or his wife's interpretation of the same event. Moreover, the family therapist might provide yet another point of departure. Still, I made no attempt to get the parties to tell the same story the same way. I asked questions; I listened.

Because of this method, the case studies remind me of the classic Japanese saga, *Rashomon*, which concerns the difficulty of pinning down the truth. In that story, a tragic event is related through the eyes of several characters; however, each person's tale significantly changes the initial picture of what happened. Consequently, *Rashomon* is not one tale. Instead, it contains as many tales as there are characters. The result: Your sympathies are swayed by each recounting of the story. Similarly, as I interviewed family members and therapists for the case histories, my perspective invariably was altered as I heard the many points of view.

In the beginning, it was not unusual for me to silently support a particular family member who later fell out of favor once I heard what someone else had to say. With time, though, the multidimensional nature of the case studies led to an ever-emerging awareness of the complex issues faced by these families, thereby helping me to understand that there are no good guys or bad guys in these situations. Personally, that insight was significant, especially when I finally figured out that it applied as well to my mistakes and my family's experiences as to anyone else's.

This book may not be a quick read, since by definition *Parents Who Help Their Children Overcome Drugs* must cover some pretty rough terrain. Therefore, don't be surprised if some chapters are more difficult to read than others because they hit home uncomfortably. If that is your experience, it's okay to temporarily skip those sections to keep moving through the material, as long as you promise yourself to go back at some point and read what you have missed. Be patient with yourself and try to accept the fact that you and your family are involved in a healing process that will take time.

❧ 1 ☙

Good Looks Are Deceiving

I was raised in what could be labeled a dysfunctional family. My father was an alcoholic, a gambler, and, on occasion, a wife beater. There were times when my mother, under stress, drank too much. Yet we were middle class by virtue of my parents' occupations: Father drove a truck for the Post Office, and Mother was a schoolteacher. We were also middle class by virtue of the image the family steadfastly presented to the local community.

We lived in a nice, well-furnished house, dressed in the latest fashions, and had an abundance of toys. However, our good looks were deceiving. As in many families, what the public observed did not quite jibe with the day-to-day reality of our household. It was not unusual, for example, for us children to return home from school and find our father and his friends engaged in a drunken brawl. Our doorbell rang at all hours of the day and night with loan sharks demanding to know why Father had not paid his debts.

We grew up—my sister, brother, and myself—admonished to keep the family secrets. We found other ways,

7

though, to act out what troubled us. To get out of the house and away from my parents, I married very young and soon had a child; my brother, who started high school enrolled in classes for exceptional students, eventually had trouble even with less challenging academic assignments; my sister soon began using drugs.

My parents' response to our individual rebellions varied. They pressured and at times punished me for my relationships with boys. They prodded my brother to improve his grades. However, my mother's typically aggressive posture did not hold up when it came to dealing with my sister's frequent use of marijuana by the time she was 15. Instead of trying to prevent it, my mother merely lamented it. The warrior on most every other front, my mother seemed helpless in the face of this unfamiliar challenge.

I did not understand the significance of what was happening to my sister; years later, I chose not to understand. My brother, the baby of the family, watched from the sidelines. My father was concerned but said nothing to my sister and little to anyone else. So the family continued to put forth its best possible face, despite our internal paralysis and inability to respond to my sister's SOS.

What I have learned in the years since is that many families, like individual people, have both public and private personas. The public persona attempts to provide an image of familial bliss or perfection. The private persona, on the other hand, reflects the authentic family dynamic, warts and all. If the private persona differs significantly from what the public is permitted to see, pressure is placed on both parents and children to maintain a false front. With time, it is inevitable that something or someone will buckle as rebellion sets in.

My sister's drug problem presented a familial blemish that would not go away. Her drug problem also represented a fissure in the family's facade. According to my sister, her use of drugs and her rebellion were fueled, at least in part, by a belief that our mother was trying to force her to be something she did not want to be. Despite good grades and high test scores, for example, my sister had no strong desire to attend college but enrolled in order to comply with our mother's expectations. Her college career lasted less than two years. Drugs and her disinterest played a role in her departure.

Clearly, my sister's behavior conflicted with the family's public persona. We were confused by the way she acted out her hostility. In retrospect, I also think we were afraid of what her acting out symbolized, what it might imply about the family's behavior. So it was easier, at least for a short time, for the family to hide behind a well-polished and well-rehearsed veneer of activity rather than to take the difficult step of admitting imperfection and then accepting the challenge to go public with my sister's problem by seeking outside help.

Ironically, mental health specialists would note that my sister's addiction could have served a very healthy function for the family had we mustered the courage to confront the problem. According to the experts, the "deviant" behavior of the child addict is frequently the stimulus that makes parents face and then accept that there is something out of line, something out of sync, with the family unit. In essence, the family is dysfunctional in some way. This type of confrontation is not a pleasant task for most parents. My family did not practice what I now preach. But, if there is a moral to this tale, it is that in the long run the challenge to change behavioral patterns, though at times uncomfortable, is a most worthwhile effort to undertake. Indeed, not to do so can be costly: No less than the good health and solid future of your child and, ultimately, your family are at stake.

THIS BOOK CAN HELP
ANY ADDICTIVE PERSONALITY

You are reading *Parents Who Help Their Children Overcome Drugs* because you either suspect or know that at least one of your children is using drugs. My sister abused marijuana and crack cocaine. Your son or daughter may have similar addictions or may be abusing a different combination of drugs. The particular drugs do not matter, in terms of how this book can be of use to you, because *Parents Who Help Their Children Overcome Drugs* will take you through a recovery process that views all substance-abusing youngsters as addictive personalities. Co-dependent family members, who adapt their behavior to accommodate the disruptions caused by the child's chemical addiction, are also considered addictive personalities. Family counselor Kathy Capell-Sowder of Dayton, Ohio, explains: "While it is commonly accepted that addiction to alcohol and drugs exists, it is less commonly understood that the person involved in a primary love relationship with someone addicted frequently displays symptoms of addiction himself in the ways that he relates to the relationship." This description of co-dependency applies as well to parents who are grappling with children who are abusing drugs. Thus, if you are a co-dependent parent this book will assist you in getting a handle on your own addictive behavior so as to minimize its effect on your troubled child.

Moreover, the book will direct you and your family

along a path that can lead to recovery. Although you will have to mobilize the courage to work for what you want, be patient with yourself and give yourself credit. After all, by having picked up this book you have already demonstrated a willingness to begin a most important journey.

THE FOUR KEY ISSUES

Parents Who Help Their Children Overcome Drugs is centered around four key issues: (1) Parents need to understand and accept the complex role they play in the lives of their substance-abusing children. (2) Parents need to learn how to help their children overcome drugs and how *not* to help. (3) Parents need to learn when it's okay to be selfish. (4) Parents need to understand the role faith plays in the recovery process.

At times these issues will overlap, because the problems under examination are interconnected. You will learn, for example, that your child's addiction is a function of your family's pathology as well as a factor in the negative dynamics your family displays (see Chapter Two, "Co-dependency—On Being Addicted to the Addict," and Chapter Three, "Hanging Tough"). My parents' dysfunctional behavior—Father's gambling and Mother's dictatorial dominance, for instance—certainly played some role in shaping the lives of my sister, brother, and myself. My sister acted out by using drugs; my brother acted out by doing poorly in school; I acted out by marrying early and by becoming a compulsive spender. On the other hand, our acts of rebellion reflected dysfunctional behavior that worked against healthy family interaction. Our antics added to the overall familial tension, which, in turn, sent my father dashing to the racetrack and led to my mother's further entrenchment into an authoritarian role: Since we were misbehaving, she felt she needed to run an even tighter ship. So, although the chapters are structured to cover separate topics, in truth, each subject is fundamentally connected to the others.

THE COMPLEX ROLE PARENTS PLAY

Admittedly, it's tough being a parent. Universities do not ordinarily provide courses in surefire techniques for successfully raising a family. The label "parent" is, by definition, complex: A mother and father are also a wife and husband and must struggle with the demands common to both roles. It is not easy being an authority figure for your children when you are a human being with foibles just like any other.

Still, there is no getting around the fact that when a person who happens to be a parent falters, the child often pays the price. When a parent develops a drinking problem, for example, behavioral patterns of broken promises and dishonesty undermine the child's confidence in the alcoholic parent and can lead to confusion, lethargy, and depression on the part of the child. Such feelings, in turn, can provoke the child to experiment with drugs in order to quell the discomfort associated with the parent's addiction to alcohol.

No family is perfect. Parents have to expect that they will make mistakes, albeit that is not an easy concept to accept. This book, through its narrative and case studies, will attempt to make that acknowledgment easier by helping you to understand the level of complexity associated with the role you as a parent play in your child's struggle with drugs. We will examine provocative questions: Is there such a thing as an addictive personality that describes your behavior as a non-drug user in terms that are similar to the behavior of your substance-abusing child? Did your bad habits contribute to your child's drug problem, or did your child's drug problem contribute to your current state of confusion and despair? Such questions are answered to some extent in this chapter and to a much larger degree in Chapter Two.

To help your child overcome drugs, another tough issue you will have to come to grips with is how to move beyond many forms of denial. For example, drug-abuse experts say that parents frequently write off the first indications of teenage drug use as "just a stage" of adolescent development. Indeed, in their book, *Loosening the Grip: A Handbook of Alcohol Information,* Jean Kinney and Gwen Leaton state that youthful alcohol abusers have been known to go as long as six years without being diagnosed.

No doubt it's hard to accept that a child, your child, is using drugs, but the truth is that the first step toward recovery—your child's, your own, and your family's— takes place when you decide to face facts, a topic that is discussed later in this chapter. Most of you who are reading *Parents Who Help Their Children Overcome Drugs* have already come this far and, thus, are ready for the next stage: learning how you can genuinely help your child.

DON'T ENABLE:
HOW TO HELP AND HOW *NOT* TO HELP

Learning how to help your child and how not to help your child is not as easy as it sounds, as demonstrated in Chapters Two on co-dependency, Four, "Raising the Bottom, or Hanging Tough Phase II," and Five, "Treatment Options." These chapters describe how parents fall into a pattern of behavior called enabling that actually works against a child's recovery process. Parents are considered enablers when they continue to rescue their children from the negative consequences of their drug-related actions.

Enablers are parents who routinely make excuses to school authorities for truant or disruptive behavior without knowing where their children actually were or what really happened. Enablers are parents who bear the expense of lawyers to help their child "beat" legal charges. Enablers are also parents who pretend that the valuables their child steals from the home to pay for drugs are simply items misplaced. Enablers consistently provide their children with "loans" that they never pay back and that go to purchase drugs.

Parents who enable are preventing their children from being connected to the consequences of their actions. By so doing, the parent is helping to undermine the child's confidence by implying that the child cannot handle her own affairs and by depriving the child of the opportunity to develop problem-solving skills. Often, the result is that the child's troublesome behavior escalates to a level that defies rescue and that carries an even stiffer price than earlier spates of wrongdoing. In truth, when you do not enable, you are treating your child with respect by displaying faith in his competence to get along in life. Treating yourself with respect is also important and sometimes requires that you display a benign form of selfishness.

IT'S OKAY TO BE SELFISH

It is possible to help your child overcome drugs and take care of yourself at the same time. Indeed, the narrative found in Chapter Three, "Hanging Tough," and in Chapter Four, "Raising the Bottom, or Hanging Tough Phase II," explains why it is sometimes necessary for you to learn how to become selfish in order to lead your child success-fully through the recovery process. There may come a time when ensuring your own well-being will require that you allow your substance-abusing child to hit bottom. Or there may come a time when you find that you have to declare your household a drug-free zone, where even cigarettes are thought of as contraband, and you must insist that family members who cannot abide by these rules must leave. Chapters Three and Four make a strong case that being the "bad guy" in the short term can really make you the good guy over the long haul, because insisting on a healthy envi-ronment for yourself helps all concerned. Being tough, however, requires strength and something less tangible but even more powerful: faith.

HAVING THE FAITH TO LET GO

Finally, parents who help their children overcome drugs have to learn how to have faith in themselves and in their children's eventual recovery. In essence, you have to de-velop faith in your sincere efforts to help your child and know that such efforts will provide a foundation of sorts that will carry the young person for many years to come. Chapter Six, "Letting Go," examines the topic of faith through the testimony of parents of children with drug problems.

FACING FACTS

Recovery, then, begins with acceptance that a drug prob-lem does in fact exist. Parents are not the only family mem-bers who have difficulty moving beyond the appearance of good looks in order to face facts about what is really happening. It may be difficult for you to get a handle on what's ailing your adolescent, for example, because of your child's instinct to deny the existence of a substance-abuse problem. Some young people, like some adults, are quite skilled at hiding their addictions.

On the other hand, your child may be unaware of her own problem with drug abuse. Los Angeles-based psychiatrist and drug counselor Loren Woodson explains, "Often teenagers themselves don't realize that their drug problem is in fact a problem." Drugs are often part of a whole constellation of problems associated with young people. For example, it might be difficult at times to determine whether abnormal behavior is caused by learning disabilities, a dysfunctional family, or drugs.

Still, you have picked up this book for a reason. Probably that reason is your concern about having noticed at least several of the following behaviors—as listed in Kinney and Leaton's *Loosening the Grip*—that lead you to believe your child is using drugs:

The emergence of secretive or isolated behavior

A significant change in personal grooming

A significant change in health, such as repeated bouts with the flu, the emergence of apparent allergic symptoms, or chronic cough or chest pains

A sudden and inexplicable drop in grades

Possession of unexplained and large sums of money, or unexplained monetary losses

The emergence of new associates to the exclusion of former close friends

Emerging problems with short-term memory

Frequent accidents

Blocks of time not accounted for

A sudden change in schedule; for example, not returning home from school at the usual time

Physical or verbal abuse of younger siblings

Unexplained mood swings

A sudden decreased interest in previously favored activities such as sports and hobbies

A sudden change in personality, demonstrating feelings of loneliness, paranoia, and depression

A sudden disappearance of possessions from the home

The discovery of drug materials and equipment among a child's belongings

Beyond assisting you in establishing that a problem with substance abuse exists in your family, *Parents Who Help Their Children Overcome Drugs* will help you to better understand your youthful drug abuser. First, don't forget how hard it is to move through adolescence. Becoming an adult is a process that involves a great deal of stress under the best of circumstances. If there is a dysfunctional element in the family already, such as an alcoholic parent, or if family members have developed the habit of not talking to each other (like that reported in Marie Brenner's *House of Dreams,* a book about the infamous Bingham family of St. Louis, whose members wrote memos to communicate), the process of growing up is even more difficult.

In a lot of cases, substance abuse is the adolescent's response to the emotional hardships encountered while trying to complete the four fundamental tasks that comprise a young person's developmental process. Kinney and Leaton describe these tasks in *Loosening the Grip.* The first task involves accepting our biological role as males and females or, more to the point, as men and women. In some circles, drug use and abuse is part of that rite of passage. Drugs can come into play, for instance, as a sort of theatrical prop—a marijuana stick dangling from a young boy's mouth, or a teenage girl leaning forward to request a light from her youthful male counterpart, supports an image of male machismo and female sophistication and seduction.

When your child begins to identify with his or her gender, it also opens up the possibility of sexual intimacy—a threatening activity at best—and brings forward the second task: learning how to be comfortable with the opposite sex. Often young people use drugs to cope with feelings of vulnerability provoked by experimentations in the sexual realm.

The struggle to attain independence is yet another developmental baptism by fire required of your child. This task, which includes going head-to-head with parents, learning how to set limits for oneself, and developing the characteristics of a healthy and prosperous adult, is an especially difficult one for young people. During this period, your child's use of drugs tests limits and rules imposed by you, the parent. The message in Chapter Three, "Hanging Tough," speaks to the hard line you may be forced to take if you are faced with these circumstances.

As your adolescent approaches his early twenties, he must face the fourth task, which is to decide on some type of occupational identity. This phase is often marked by many false starts and thus "failures," as viewed by the adolescent. The great pressure associated with the need to succeed and the desire to break familial ties and move on can lead to heavy drug abuse.

What these four developmental stages do not explain is why, though every child experiences some of the discomfort connected with the completion of these tasks, not every child deals with it by using drugs. I experimented with some drugs as a child and as an adult, but for some reason I chose not to act out my rebellion by becoming a substance abuser. My sister, however, took a different route. You may have one child who uses drugs and two children who do not. Why that happens is not known, though some drug-abuse experts speculate that there may be a genetic predisposition for substance abuse and compulsive behavior that surfaces in one child and not in another of the same family.

What we do know, which parents need to face, is this. Becoming an adult is generally a pretty tough process to move through, and some young people try to cope by succumbing to drugs. Chapter Two, "Co-dependency—On Being Addicted to the Addict," discusses more thoroughly how parents can prepare their children to successfully handle the stresses and strains that are a part of this natural developmental process.

FROM HOPELESSNESS
TO HELP IN THREE STAGES

As a parent you try your best to fulfill your responsibility for the loving guidance of your child. Still, you are not perfect, as your child is not perfect. Try to keep that in mind as you turn the pages of this book and move from a position of helplessness to knowledge that there are things you can do to help your child.

The following three-stage scenario broadly describes the progression that ordinarily takes place within a dysfunctional family made more dysfunctional by having to cope with a young drug abuser. Not all families move through each stage. Some families get stuck in the first or second stages. Others experience all three stages only to fall prey again to the same behavioral patterns that fed the dysfunction in the first place. The bottom line is that the pathology between your drug-using child and the role you have played in your child's life cuts both ways. Still, just as you and your child share the "ailment," you and your child can recover by understanding the process that you both are going through and by working together to overcome the problems related to substance abuse and co-dependency.

EARLY STAGE: "SOLVING" THE PROBLEM

As a child's experimentation with drugs becomes an addiction, a parent's awareness typically moves from an all-encompassing denial that nothing bad is really happening, to a modified denial that seeks to establish a new set of standards for what is the norm. You make excuses to explain deviations in your child's pattern of behavior, and you describe gross deviations as isolated incidents, nothing to worry about.

In time, however, even the most blind parental eye comes to recognize that the child is in trouble. At that time, the parent makes an attempt to "solve" the drug-abuse problem by protecting the family and the dysfunctional member from external encroachment and ridicule. You may cover up for the substance abuser by making excuses to school authorities for truancy, for example, or by lying to other family members and friends about what is really going on. Unfortunately, such enabling tactics allow the child's behavior to continue unchecked, supporting rather than eradicating the symptoms of drug abuse. Enabling prevents the abuser from experiencing the pain and disruption that would signal there is something wrong in her life.

Enabling also prevents the family from facing its overall problems.

MIDDLE STAGE: ADAPTING TO ADDICTION

Normal efforts to eliminate the problem simply do not work. As the situation worsens with the substance-abusing child, the family's level of frustration and sense of failure increase as well. Still, during this period families tend to try even harder to help, although their efforts have not worked and will not work. Such families feed their own frustration by believing that the reason their children remain in trouble has something to do with the parents not making enough effort. So they try harder by literally taking on the responsibilities of the adolescent drug abuser, such as doing homework that has not been completed or paying for unpaid parking tickets, lost school books, or damaged cars.

CHRONIC STAGE: SINKING INTO CHAOS

At this stage the family has sincerely tried everything it knows to help the substance-abusing child and has failed, because virtually all of the family's attempts can be classified as enabling activities. Guilt, despair, and chaos are most often the outward expressions of that sense of failure. The family no longer believes in its ability to solve the problem. The only recourse is to seek outside help.

Though I have painted this progression in bleak terms, at every stage the opportunity for recovery exists for both the family and the affected child. As ensuing chapters and case studies will demonstrate, parents can indeed learn how to challenge and change old patterns of destructive behavior; adolescent drug abusers can also learn how to challenge and change their behavior patterns in a constructive and healthy manner. So, how do parents start to help their children overcome drugs? They can begin by turning the pages of this book slowly and by paying careful attention to the tales shared by parents, and sometimes the young abusers themselves, who have traveled the same road on which they are about to embark. The following case study provides one such opportunity to learn about the process of recovery.

On the face of it, this family is deceptively good-looking, a prototypical middle-class, suburban household: The husband is the primary wage earner, the wife has been a housewife during most of the marriage, and the three offspring are attractive children who, according to the mother, "have never really wanted for anything." Yet the oldest child has been using marijuana and cocaine for a number of years, though he is only 20.

CASE STUDY:
SHARON, JOHN, AND AARON

Sharon's voice quavers at times when she talks about her 20-year-old son, Aaron. Sharon, 44, describes the last seven years of her life as "living in hell" because of what she has experienced while trying to cope with her son's drug habit. A housewife, Sharon has been supported financially by her husband, John, for most of the 23 years they have been married. However, she feels she has not received emotional backup from John in dealing with Aaron's drug problems.

John, 45, takes a stoic and more hard-line approach when he discusses Aaron's recent past, although there are signs that he worries, as does Sharon, about what will

become of Aaron. "The wife and I deal with things differently. I wasn't asleep when Aaron was doing some of the
things he was doing. She just thinks I was sleeping."

In addition to Aaron, Sharon and John have two
daughters—Monique, 22, and Nicole, 19. This is a home-
owning, middle-class family living in a suburban section of
Los Angeles that was once farmland. Today, many of the
neighborhood streets are populated by teenage dope dealers, who make most of their money through the sale of
cocaine. Sharon and John know a lot about this life because
of John's occupation—he heads a program that finds jobs
for economically disadvantaged young people—and because their son spent many a night on these streets selling
crack cocaine in order to support his own habit.

SHARON

Sharon looks tired as she explains that the past seven years
have produced nightmare experiences. She describes a
scene where Aaron was in the middle of the street and a
woman, screaming that Aaron had sold her some "bunk"
dope and she wanted her money back, held a knife to his
neck. On another occasion, Sharon was in her kitchen
cooking when Aaron, closely followed by a knife-wielding
youngster, burst into the back door and led a chase through
the first floor of the family's home.

According to Sharon, these experiences only begin to
tell of the pain, uncertainty, and worry that started when
Aaron was only 13. At that time, in 1981, Sharon received
a call from her husband reporting that Aaron had been
caught using marijuana with friends. She was dismayed by
the news, Sharon says, but she had "expected that this day
would come."

Over the years, their neighborhood had changed, and

Sharon was concerned. Some of the local children who were Aaron's age had older brothers and sisters in jail. "Aaron's best friend's brother had been in jail. And Aaron was very attached to this kid because Aaron didn't have a brother," she explains. She wanted to get Aaron out of the neighborhood—to enroll him in a private school or to uproot the entire family and move. But, she reports, with a note of bitterness in her voice, "John said no." Her husband's rationale was that their family should stay and become the "leaders of the community. It seems to me that John wants us [the family] to be community leaders at any cost."

Her husband was motivated to remain in the community because of the way he was raised. "John's family was the most well-off family of the local community. John had many more opportunities and economic advantages than the other kids in the neighborhood, and he was resented for having so much more and ridiculed for being made by his parents to go to music classes and things like that." The result, Sharon points out, is that John has rebelled against his upbringing in a number of ways. He uses colloquial language, for example, and he refuses to move away from the community in which they currently live.

So they stayed, and by the time Aaron was 16 he had been introduced to cocaine. Sharon explains: "One of Aaron's friends was dating a woman about eight years his senior. This girlfriend would invite the neighborhood boys over and supply them with marijuana cigarettes laced with a crystal-type substance that I later found out was crack cocaine. If I had known the danger of it, I would have put my foot down. I would have really watched Aaron's every movement. But, at the time, I didn't know that some people can get addicted to crack almost immediately."

During this period, Aaron, a child who had been

placed in classes for the mentally gifted while in elementary school, was arrested for the first time. He was caught stealing expensive bicycles from racks at the local college, delivering the contraband to a man in the neighborhood who paid Aaron and his buddies $20 for their efforts. Sharon was puzzled by the phone call from the police station. "We're not rich or anything, but my kids were not deprived," she says, so why would Aaron need to steal? Sharon and John later discovered that Aaron's cocaine habit was what motivated him to steal, including objects that belonged to members of the household. However, it took another example of abnormal behavior before Sharon and John really understood that their son was addicted to cocaine and how that addiction was damaging his life.

After that first arrest, things rapidly went from bad to worse. "He started ditching school at around the same time he started stealing, and he had never been rebellious at school. Then, besides missing his classes, Aaron started coming home later and later. He also started coming home with a lot of money in his pockets." Soon the family heard rumors that their son was spending his evenings selling drugs on one of the local streets. The tales were confirmed one day when a man in his mid-thirties, who had served time for murder and was known as a recruiter of children to sell drugs, knocked on the door looking for Aaron. Sharon says, "When we demanded to know what this guy wanted with Aaron, he told us, 'I put money in Aaron's pocket.' " Aaron's explanation: "I've made some deliveries for him."

From that moment forward, Sharon reports, her nightmare odyssey began. "I went to the street and actually saw Aaron hailing cars down to sell drugs. All of this started in 1985, a few months before his seventeenth birthday. So every night his sisters and I would get in the family truck and zoom down this street and make Aaron come home. He would hide in the bushes or behind a tree to avoid us. After a while, he was able to recognize the truck by its missing headlight, so I starting driving down the street with the lights out on the truck in order to fool him. Once I even brought a baseball bat with me to use as a threat to make sure Aaron got in the truck to go home. Every night the girls and I went after him. And we never came home without him.

"It got so that I was a nervous wreck, because I was keeping the same hours as Aaron. I was out all night most every night. My oldest daughter also suffered because she was the one who went with me most of the time. My husband slept through it all." Sharon kept trying, because she couldn't give up on her son. In addition, "A few times he told me he couldn't help it, that he was hooked on the drugs and couldn't help himself."

A year after Aaron's initial involvement with crack, he was in a near-fatal automobile accident. Because he had traces of cocaine in his blood, the medication that could save his life wasn't working as well as it should have. He did recover, and for about the first 30 days after his return from the hospital, "Aaron was a model son at first. He was clean of dope. He helped around the house. He was sweet. He was the son that he used to be. When he got his insurance settlement from the accident he was very generous and started buying neighborhood people presents.

"Around that time someone in the neighborhood decided to reintroduce Aaron to crack to get more money from him. And this time when Aaron became addicted, he was completely out of control. He would put his fist through walls when he didn't get what he wanted, or scream and holler when things didn't go his way." It didn't take Aaron long to run through his insurance settlement, which sent him back into the streets to obtain the money to support his drug habit.

This time, Aaron's drug-dealing activities took place in the front yard of the home. "I asked him not to run the streets because of what had happened to him as a result of the car accident," Sharon says, "so he starting selling cocaine in front of the house. Cars would drive up at all hours of the night. I would stand out front and take license plate numbers and threaten to turn the buyers in to the police. I would argue with the guys who were standing in my front yard purchasing the dope. John stayed in bed. I really believe that if a man, my husband, had been outside doing what I was doing, he could have put a stop to the dope traffic. But my efforts didn't keep the thugs away."

Eventually, Aaron sold cocaine to an undercover police officer and was arrested. He was released to enter a drug treatment center. Aaron lasted a few days in one treatment facility, a month in another, and finally settled in a long-term (six to nine months) residential treatment program that appears to be a good fit. Sharon's never-say-die attitude about her son's drug problems was strengthened by thoughts she had had after Aaron's close bout with death: "After the accident I used to think, 'Is Aaron going to die without having known what it felt like to live a full and clean life?' I began to think, 'If he were dead, how would I help some other kid in a position similar to Aaron's before his death?' And then whatever ideas I came up with, I would transfer the thoughts to Aaron by pointing out to myself that he was still alive.

"Every time Aaron was in trouble, everyone wanted us to use 'tough love' tactics. Everyone wanted Aaron put out into the streets, including my husband, but I wouldn't let John do that, even though sometimes I thought about it. Drug dealers *want* kids to be put out on the streets.

Besides, I believed I should keep trying because you've never tried everything. Now Aaron thanks me for not giving up on him."

JOHN

"It ain't so much where you live, but how you live where you live," says John, who has a bachelor of arts degree in behavioral science, in explaining why he refused to allow the family to leave the area even after it became difficult to pull Aaron away from a local crowd that used and sold drugs. Unlike Sharon, John doesn't blame the neighborhood for their son's problems: "The neighborhood hoodlums didn't come out in front of the house except for what Aaron brought in front of the house. It ain't the neighborhood, it's what Aaron was doing in the neighborhood that was the problem." Besides, John adds, "I came from a background where I stayed in a house that I grew up in all of my life, so I don't like moving." John, Sharon, and the children have lived in the same house for 20 years.

"At first I didn't want to believe Aaron was on crack," John recalls. "But then our camera, tools, jewelry, anything that couldn't be nailed to the floor, was stolen from the home. Aaron was arrested for selling cocaine, he was convicted of armed robbery. . . . Sharon feels I don't have any confidence in Aaron. But it's just that I know what that cocaine can do to you and I believe that it takes a superperson to overcome this. I don't know that Aaron is a superperson. In fact, I don't know anyone who is a superperson."

These days, John thinks a lot about the impact Aaron's ordeal has had on himself, Sharon, and their two daughters. "I wasn't asleep when the old lady was out in the middle of the night chasing Aaron. You can't sleep during that kind of situation. But you can't stay up all night either, because you have to get up in the morning. What I had to deal with was, I was the only one working. Sharon spent so much time trying to handle Aaron's problem, she neglected everything and everyone else, including me."

On the other hand, he says, "Sharon was a punching bag. If she took Aaron's side, I got angry. If she took my side, Aaron got angry. I bet she wondered, 'If these are the two men in my life that love me, I don't need any enemies.' What I feel good about, though, was how the girls dealt with the problem. No matter how angry they were about having their personal belongings stolen by their brother, they always felt that they could get another necklace, but their brother had a problem." John does admit, however, that his oldest daughter still stays up most of the night from having spent so many evenings roaming the streets with her mother in search of her brother.

When asked what he thinks of Sharon's comment that the price paid for the family to stay in the community and maintain a position of leadership may have been too high, John says, "I think about that now and then." In a quieter voice, he adds, "Sometimes I wonder if she's right."

AARON

"All of my friends were doing it [using drugs], so I started doing it, too," explains 20-year-old Aaron, speaking during his second month at a long-term residential drug treatment center. Aaron is quick to point out, however, that peer-group pressure was only one of two reasons he started smoking marijuana at 14 or 15. The other reason: "I had a good time when I used drugs; I had fun."

Aaron's "good times" continued after he entered high school, when his substance abuse expanded to include alcohol. "There was a park near my high school where we would hang out and get high. I started ditching classes to drink beer and smoke marijuana." According to Aaron, his parents became alerted to the fact that something was wrong as his school attendance declined significantly. After a while he simply stopped going to school.

His parents had very different attitudes about what should be done. "My mother would say stuff like, 'Not my son. He's not using drugs.' Now my father, he knew what was going on and wanted to ground me, but my mother had the final say-so and wouldn't let him do anything to me." Meanwhile, Aaron's habit grew to include cocaine by the eleventh grade, when the older girlfriend of one of his buddies introduced him and other teenage boys to a marijuana stick laced with cocaine, which she called a primo.

Puffing on a primo produced a feeling unlike anything Aaron had previously experienced. "I got a rush from smoking it. I can't explain any better than that how good it felt. I just can't explain it." His addiction to primos sent him out into the streets in desperate search of money. Approximately five primos could be derived from one cocaine rock, and one rock at that time cost $25. To meet such expenses, he reports, "I had to start doing things to get my money together to pay for the four to six primos I was smoking a day. So I started snatching purses, stealing car radios, doing little things like that."

As he smoked more, his tolerance for primos increased and thus he needed to smoke even more to feel the rush. When he developed a $50-a-day habit, his criminal activities escalated to include breaking into homes and strong-armed robberies. Aaron's voice drops to a whisper as he explains what strong-armed robbery is: "It's when you beat up people and steal from them." When Aaron's consumption of primos reached the $400-a-day range, he turned to selling cocaine. He would pick up a sack filled with $500 worth of cocaine, which the supplier would provide on credit, providing Aaron returned $300 in sales within a certain time. The $200 profit margin was Aaron's cut for dealing dope.

Aaron traveled from street to street selling cocaine, changing locations only when a particular avenue became "hot" with police infestation. Eventually he was caught by the authorities but not, at first, for his drug activities. "I finally got popped by the police for a strong-armed robbery." Aaron and a few friends had decided to rob a woman. In the process of snatching her purse, one of the boys hit her, though Aaron says that it was not he. They got caught when the driver of their getaway car drove down a dead-end street, giving bystanders time to take down the license number. Later the same evening, a detective knocked on Aaron's door and he was arrested.

Three months later Aaron was in a near-fatal car accident. He and a friend had been getting high off cocaine all day and drinking. The accident occurred when his friend tried to drive onto a main highway, lost control of the car, and ran into a rail. Aaron flew out the back window. He was on the critical list for two months, in a coma for six weeks of that time. When he came out of the coma he was paralyzed from the neck down. He did regain his physical mobility in a few days, but it took longer for his memory to be restored—about a month.

"The doctors had told my mother that they didn't think I was going to make it. And if I did make it, they said I wouldn't remember anybody for at least eight years. But through the grace of God, everything started coming back. They had psychiatrists working with me and I was doing all of this work on computers and stuff." Computer puzzles and games were used to test how much of his capacity to remember remained. But, he adds, "Before they would release me from the hospital, I had a meeting with all the specialists and all the doctors and they told me, 'Aaron, we know you're an addict.' I looked at them like they were crazy. I said, 'What are you talking about?' I had forgotten all of this. So they told me that if I continued to use cocaine once I got out, I could probably have a relapse.

"My accident caused me to have a lot of swelling around the brain and they had to drain it. They said that cocaine is a drug that goes straight to the brain. And they said that that [using cocaine] could possibly cause the swelling to start again and that I might not be so fortunate the next time. So I got out of the hospital and I wasn't messing around with any drugs or drinking. Then I got my $50,000 settlement from the accident and I was doing good. But then one of my friends had this sick idea that we were going to become rich by selling cocaine. So I started back selling cocaine again and I was making a lot of money."

Along with his return to the streets to deal dope, Aaron began to drink and "smoke a little marijuana." He was not using cocaine at first. "But one of my so-called partners, who wasn't in the car with me selling the cocaine and who wasn't making all the money I was making, asked me if I wanted a Buddha Thai joint [an especially potent type of marijuana]. I said, 'Yeah,' and stuck it in my top pocket. Later on that night I went outside to smoke it, and I lit it up and I took a puff and I said, 'Damn, this don't taste like no Buddha Thai.' And then I smelled it and it smelled kind of good. Then I took a big hit and I blew it out and I said, 'Oh my God, this is a primo.' "

At that moment, Aaron got scared and threw the primo to the ground and ran into his home acting paranoid he says, because he didn't know what to do. "So I called up my girl and I told her I was going to come get her and then go get a motel room. Then I went and picked up a half-ounce of cocaine. When I got to the room I smoked up about half of that half-ounce and then I called my partner up, and we stayed there about a day and a half just smoking cocaine. My cocaine habit started back right then."

This time, Aaron had so much money from selling cocaine that he moved quickly to an expensive primo dependency. "When I first started [smoking primos] after I got out of the hospital, I was spending about $200 every now and then on cocaine. Then it started to be $200 just about every day. Then it was $200 or $300 every day. My father was aware of what was going on, so they stopped giving me my [settlement] money. But then I had to start selling drugs again because they weren't giving me my money. If I had a bad day and didn't earn much, I would still ask my father or my mother for some money, but they would say no. So I started stealing from home. I never used to steal from home, but, see, I'd bought a lot of gifts for them. So I said, 'Well, I bought you all of this stuff and you can't give me any money?' And they said, 'No, Aaron. We know what you're doing with it.' So I started stealing from home." When he couldn't generate enough funds from what he took from his family, Aaron returned to the streets with a vengeance.

"It got to the point where I was back on the streets selling dope every day. Then I hooked back up with my partner, and together we were totally smoked out. We were smoking $600 or $700 a day. After a while, I got tired of walking to other places to sell the cocaine, so we turned our street into a dope street. The police became aware of what we were doing. The neighbors became aware of what we were doing. My father was aware of what we were doing, and my mother finally came around to being aware of what we were doing."

Aaron's father told him he knew Aaron was an addict and asked if he wanted help to overcome his problem with drugs. "I said no. So my father said, 'Well, if you're going to do it [sell and use drugs], keep the shit away from my house.' So we would walk down the street and sell, but when it got late, I used to stand out in front of the house." Soon he was arrested for possession of cocaine with intent to sell. In exchange for doing some undercover work for the police department, Aaron got off with no time served and only two years' probation. The experience caused him to stop selling drugs in front of his home, but it did not cause him to stop smoking cocaine, although he did reduce his habit to "only about $75 a day."

This time, to support his addiction, Aaron and his friends started manufacturing phony cocaine, which they sold to unsuspecting clients as the real thing. "We started beating people out of their money. We would get some Monterey jack cheese and then leave it on the roof for about a week. Then we would cut it up and let the cheese rocks sit for a while in the oral gel that you put on your teeth. Then we would take the pieces out and let them dry out and get hard. When that happened, the cheese would look just like rocks of cocaine. One day I sold $400 worth of it. People would come back and I would deny that I had even sold them that, and by that time I would have real cocaine, so I would give them a little piece of mine, so they would end up buying some more. It was a crazy game."

Aaron has since discovered that his volatile life impacted his parents' life in an equally volatile way. "I found out in here [the residential treatment center] that they [parents] go through the same states of depressions that we do. My mother was to the point where she was asking herself, 'Why me? What did I do wrong? I thought I raised him right.' She got to the point where she just cut me off. She believed that I was going to do what I wanted to do, and all that she could do was pray for me."

Around this time, Aaron called his probation officer, after not having reported as required for about two months. The conversation was a sobering one: "My probation officer said, 'Sorry, buddy, I've turned you in. I made a recommendation that you go to the state penitentiary.' He said he was tired of seeing guys like me take advantage of their families. He felt that the only way for me to see the light was to do some time, some long time. So I panicked and told my mom. We were almost to the point where I was going to go to Canada and stay with some relatives up there, because I didn't want to go to the penitentiary.

"I talked to my father and he said, 'They're going to catch you anyway, you've got to come back sooner or later.' So I called my lawyer and he told me that the only thing I probably had going for me was if I got into a long-term [treatment] program, because usually if you get into a program they won't snatch you out to take you to jail. So I went to this one program up in Lancaster in the middle of the desert. But I was the youngest person there, everybody else was about thirty-five and up. So I really didn't fit in, I didn't feel comfortable. I called my mom and dad and told them that I was doing good, that I was praying and everything, then the next day I called them and told them that I was out of the program, that I couldn't take it. So my father picked me up and took me home. I had been clean about ten days, so I was looking better—the bags under my eyes had started to go away. The first day I was back my mom bought me all types of little things and I didn't mess with any drugs that day, I just hung around the house watching videos."

Trouble started the next day, however. As Aaron sat outside the house with his sisters, a former cocaine client drove up and waited to see if Aaron would serve him. "This guy was a guy who always spent like a hundred or more dollars. So I was thinking to myself, 'Should I do it?' I didn't know if I should because I had been clean. But I said, '——— it,' and I ran out to the car with him and I heard my sister screaming, 'Mommy, Mommy, Mommy!'

"So I went back and stood at the side of the house and I smoked a primo. Then I went inside the house and I saw my sister crying. Then I walked down the hallway and I saw my dad, who said, 'Go look and see what you've done to your mother.' And I thought, 'Damn, what did I do? What did I do?' So I went back there and she was just in a hysterical condition. She was crying and crying and she wouldn't talk to me. So I went into my room and I started crying. When I came out, my other sister said that she hated me; my father slammed me to the wall and told me that my mother had to go to the hospital because of what I had done to her. So I got this idea. I got my father's keys to his office where I knew he kept a gun. I got the gun, hopped into my car, and went to the nearest park. I was crying and everything, thinking, 'Why am I here? I just messed up my whole family. I'm the cause of all of these problems.' I decided to kill myself. I pulled the cock back, but the clip wasn't in the gun. So I thought to myself, 'Damn, there must really be a God.' "

Aaron returned home that evening to a calmer environment. He was able to talk to his mother, and the next day he entered the program he is in now. He has been clean ever since—at the time of this interview, approximately 120 days. It feels good, he says, for a number of reasons. "I want to stay clean now because I'm back to where I can talk to my father. He respects me now. He doesn't call me names and stuff. And my sisters like me. Well, they always liked me, but now I can see the love in everybody." These days, Aaron says that he has some goals he wants to achieve.

"I'm not a dumb person. I want to take some courses in public speaking, I want to get my high school diploma, and I want to work with my father."

POSTSCRIPT

According to his drug counselor, Barbara Green of the Pomona, California-based American Hospital, Aaron has come a long way in the two-and-a-half months he has been in this program. "The Aaron that's sitting across from me now is attempting to become humble, trusting, open-minded, and is in touch with himself and his feelings," she says. "The Aaron that I met when he first came into this program was a very angry, hostile, nontrusting individual."

Most of what Aaron has yet to achieve, Green says, centers around problems with his co-dependent family, especially his mother. "Aaron has walked through a lot of pain in his life already," Green notes, "but right now he has to find a way to feel like an accomplished person so that he can leave this program and become a productive member of society without relying on his mother as much as he does now. We call it detachment with love—that's what we're trying to help him with now."

Both Aaron and his mother are involved in multi-family therapy groups. It's turning out to be more difficult for his mother to detach than for Aaron, Green reports. "I thought it would be the other way around. But it's proving to be real tough on his mother." When Aaron first arrived and Green told him he needed to take a look at the co-dependency issue between himself and his mother, that he needed to break away, Aaron resisted mightily. "He was still in his bad-head stage and believed that all I wanted to do was make him stop loving his mom. But that wasn't it at all. I just wanted him to grow up."

Green considers it a good sign, then, that Aaron is talking more and more about how he wants to get to know his father better. This suggests Aaron is moving in the right direction, because his father is a "tough-love type of guy."

"To be honest with you," Green says, "Aaron is the one case that I thought I would have the most trouble with. What I think happened is that early on Aaron called one of his peers here a punk. That kind of language is unacceptable. So I give him a discipline, which is a learning experience. I gave him a topic to write about on respect and that's when the change happened here."

The day she gave Aaron that assignment, she recalls, he was very upset with her and the entire program. "His peers took him out into the back parking lot and walked him around and just let him vent his anger. At that time Aaron wanted to leave the program. His peers told him that staying in the program was what he needed to do; however, it was his decision. If he wanted to remain a sick person and not get better, that was his choice also."

Green offers the following thoughts as to why Aaron responded with such anger to a relatively mild reprimand: "I can only tell you what my gut tells me, and that is I think Aaron—who knew exactly what buttons to push around his mother, an enabler, to make her respond the way she did—was really angry with me for making him take a look at that behavior and angry with himself for having taken advantage of his mother's enabling behavior for so long."

At this point in the recovery process, Green gives Aaron a prognosis of "fair" in terms of overcoming his chemical dependencies. To that end, Green is working with Aaron to help him find a place to stay outside his home community, Pomona. "Aaron has already told me that he does not want to remain in Pomona, and I am helping him explore other possibilities, including going into the service—an idea his mother doesn't like. She wants him to return to the home. But we're working on her— that's why we have multifamily group therapy."

Aaron's mother still worries about what will happen when he gets out of the treatment program. But, she feels, "It's my duty as a parent to do everything I can to help Aaron, and to never, never, never give up." Aaron's father is also apprehensive about how Aaron will fare when he is released, but his thoughts focus more on what new rules should be established for Aaron to live by. Explains John: "He's never really had to work. My thing is, if you're going to live here [in the family home], you're going to have to live by my rules, and that includes getting a job. I love my son very much, but I want him to become his own man."

At a recent multifamily group therapy session, the parents were asked to write down what they really wanted to see change in their relationship with their substance-abusing child. Most of the parents, John explains, came up with statements such as they wanted to "improve communications." However uncomfortable it made him, John opted to make a more provocative comment. "This may sound selfish," he told the other parents, "but what I'd like is for my kids to become more independent, to start doing something on their own. I want some peace and quiet for myself, and I want some quality time with my wife."

John also admitted to the group that he still broods about some of the activities Aaron got involved in when he was using drugs. "There's a lot of hostility and anger in me about what he did. So it's going to take more than a couple of months of Aaron being in this program before I'm going to forget about what he put our family through."

Do Sharon and John need treatment in order to better deal with their son? Sharon has been labeled a co-dependent. Is John? Have Sharon and John enabled Aaron to live the drug-related lifestyle he led for so many years? Chapter Two, "Co-dependency—On Being Addicted to the Addict," sorts out the questions raised by the experiences of this couple.

ℳ *2* ℳ

Co-dependency —On Being Addicted to the Addict

For years I helped my sister use drugs by refusing to acknowledge that there was something wrong and by at times adapting my lifestyle, and consequently the rules that ordinarily governed my life, to her addictive behavior. My way was to simply not see, as had been our father's way as well.

Our parents separated when my sister was nearly 14 and I was 24 and away at college. My sister opted to live with my father, who worked the night shift. Her involvement with drugs began during that period: Most evenings, she left the house shortly after Father left for work.

She explains, "Dad and I never discussed where I was or what I did when he was at work. Dad may have surmised, Dad may have presumed, but Dad didn't *know* because he never asked." Part of the problem in communications stemmed from the fact that my mother and father were going through a bitter divorce and Father viewed my sister as a miniature of my mother.

According to my sister, "Dad saw more and more of

41

Mom in me. So he just resented me more and more. He never dealt with me on my own level, and Mom didn't deal with me at all, so I was alone. All I had were my friends." In an attempt to escape the unpleasantness of her life, she turned to drugs. "I liked getting high," she recalls, "but the high isn't what kept me doing it—it was the escape that went along with the process of getting high. I didn't have anyone, so that's what I was turned on to, the escape."

Soon my sister's nighttime activities began to interfere with her day. She became more and more lethargic. She slept during the day and often remained home from school. Though all signs pointed to drug or alcohol abuse, my father never pressed her for answers; he never asked what was causing her to change.

My turn came some years later when my sister, then 26, moved in with me. By then she was addicted to crack or rock cocaine. At best I can say I didn't know her problems were drug related, at least not initially. At worst I can say I suspected as much but really didn't want to know. Even now, I'm still not clear which is true, but I can admit these days that the way I adapted to her abnormal behavior allowed her addiction to flourish.

One of the first ways I covered for her was financially. Though she worked every day, she seldom seemed to have any money. In the beginning, I thought a lot about why that was so, but I eventually made excuses for her monetary shortages and paid the bills myself.

Another way I adapted to her addiction was to dutifully report to other family members and friends how well she was doing. I worked on the assumption that to tell the truth about my sister's personal affairs would somehow betray her, that what she did was her own business and should not be reported to others. Moreover, I played the same game with her as had my father years earlier: It was not until the very end of her stay with me that I even questioned her about her use of drugs. Like my father, I avoided asking the hard questions. In retrospect, I believe I did what I did because I had many of the same feelings that my sister reports having felt. In essence, had I discussed her "problem" with others as well as with her, I would have had to confront the fact that I was as out of control in my life as she was in hers, and that I felt as isolated and as helpless as she.

Not surprisingly, my behavior enabled my sister's behavior to become worse. It was not long before she could not catch up with her debts. Soon she was disappearing for days at a time, and when she did return home it was obvious that she was wide-eyed and "wired" from drugs.

Still, I did not request that she leave my home. Instead, I paid the bills and continued to provide her with a haven where she was guaranteed shelter, food, and unlimited use of a phone, and where no questions were asked. I resented her, however, and her attitude suggested she resented me. We barely spoke to each other. When she was home, she stayed sequestered in her bedroom most of the time. I begrudged her use of the telephone. I begrudged her trips to the refrigerator. In general, I begrudged her very presence. Yet I never said a word to her about my anger and frustration or about what I was finally beginning to suspect: My sister was an abuser of drugs.

Experts now consider such capitulation to an addict's behavior an illness in its own right. My behavior was typical of the co-dependent. I was addicted to my sister's addictive behavior. As defined by Sharon Wegscheider-Cruse, a California-based drug-abuse counselor, co-dependency "is a primary disease. . . . It is what happens to family members when they try to adapt to a sick family system that seeks to protect and enable the alcoholic [or drug-dependent person]. Each family member enters into this collusion in his own individual way."

As is always the case, my co-dependent behavior hurt myself as well as my sister. For example, I have since learned that I was motivated to "protect" my sister's image from family and friends in order to assume a position of control over my sister's life. By so doing, I hoped, on some unconscious level, that my sister would feel grateful and thus owe me allegiance. The point of this elaborate ruse of exercising control was that I needed to feel needed, even if to do so required my sister's emotional subjugation. Such co-dependent behavior on my part impaired my sister's already low self-esteem, since the message I sent to her was: You must be a bad person, because to upgrade your image I have to tell a bunch of lies.

So, as a co-dependent person, I fed on my sister's abnormal behavior. To some extent my sister fed just as heavily on my co-dependent responses to her drug-related actions. What we became, then, were two members of an unhealthy team who played the same destructive game over and over again.

Parents who want to help their children overcome drugs have to learn how to break that cycle. The chapters that follow cover how to accomplish this, bringing up such matters as "hanging tough"—learning when and how to draw the line—in addition to approaches to treatment options for parents and their troubled children.

PORTRAIT OF A CO-DEPENDENT

As a parent of a child who abuses drugs, you may already recognize yourself as a co-dependent personality. You have probably felt it your responsibility to maintain the family's equilibrium, knocked out of kilter by your child's chemical dependency. As a co-dependent, it's likely that you have tried to take on the responsibilities abandoned by your child, such as doing her neglected homework or paying for dented fenders caused by her driving under the influence of alcohol or drugs. Sometimes you've lied to protect your child, your family, and (not least) your psyche. Often you've vacillated from entirely accepting the "blame" for your child's chemical dependency to projecting the blame onto someone else or something else that will not or cannot refute the allegation. My father, for example, died when my sister was 16. It is much easier for my mother (and, I must admit, myself at times) to blame my father for many of the family's ills than to share in that blame.

According to Jael Greenleaf, president of Los Angeles-based Greenleaf & Associates, an organization that specializes in conducting workshops for adult children of alcoholics, additional co-dependent behaviors include:

An Inflated Sense of Self

By living your own life as well as taking over the day-to-day responsibilities abandoned by your drug-abusing child, you feel that you are a superhuman person. Yet because you are hoping to exact a price of emotional subservience from your child in return for your efforts to "save" her, the bionic image you maintain of yourself is tainted by the feeling of martyrdom.

Distrust of Your Child

Often, when faced with a child who is using drugs, parents naively believe that they have the power to personally and quickly make their child stop substance abuse, or they think that the child himself can stop on his own without help. The child may fuel that belief by promising time and time again that he has broken the habit, only to start up again. Children who feel compelled to offer such false promises have to lie about many other activities to hide the fact that they are still using drugs. Eventually, co-dependent parents learn to distrust their children.

A Tendency to Lie

Some co-dependent parents who learn to live with the lies their sons and daughters tell also begin to tell lies themselves to support what they want to believe about their children. Parents lie as well to "protect" their children from exposure. Whatever motivates the lie, being dishonest typically produces guilt in the parent and child, though they rarely acknowledge the guilt.

A Judgmental Attitude Toward Others

Co-dependent parents tend to find fault with children of other families, with their neighborhood, with their spouses, with most anything and anyone except themselves. They display this type of behavior in order to deflect attention from the so-called failure of their family, exemplified by a drug-abusing child. Severe and continual judgment of others that stems from a feeling of isolation further perpetuates that feeling.

Solitariness

Feeling helpless and unable to change their children's behavior often causes co-dependent parents to feel like failures and to feel ashamed of that perceived failure. So they withdraw and become antisocial. Sometimes they act out such behavior in a way that causes them to appear snobbish. They may start to shun longtime friends of the family, for example.

Depression

Feeling down-and-out is considered "the common cold of psychopathology." Basically, depression is fueled by loss. Co-dependent parents feel a loss of legitimate power over their troubled children. Parents who have made plans for the futures of their sons and daughters become frustrated and finally despondent as they watch their substance-abusing children slowly self-destruct.

Do you recognize yourself in this portrait of a co-dependent? I saw myself among these examples, and once I got over the shock, I began to take steps to redraw the portrait. You can use this information, as I did, to start a self-enlightenment process. Just reading the list of co-dependent behaviors helped me to become aware of the self-defeating ways I acted out my feelings of frustration, helplessness, and fear.

First, I made it a point to take note of my co-dependent reactions to family members and friends. I didn't try to alter my behavior in the beginning; I just tried to pay close attention so that I could understand what or who was more or less likely to trigger a co-dependent response from me. Later, I would imagine other ways I might have responded to the same circumstance. With time, I developed the courage to experiment with other, more healthy, behavioral approaches. Nowadays, I still slip into co-dependent patterns of behavior, but less frequently than before.

Thus, by redrawing your own portrait of co-dependency, you can gain more control over your life while becoming less manipulative of others. An added benefit of redrawing your portrait is that you will become less vulnerable to the manipulative behavior of your substance-abusing child. Indeed, as the next section points out, it is all too easy for parents of children who use drugs to fall victim to the addictive-personality syndrome, where mother, father, and child alike feed on each other's co-dependencies.

LOSING CONTROL/GAINING CONTROL

As your child becomes more and more dependent on drugs, she will play out a downward spiral that can end with her having lost control of her life while gaining control of yours. Under such circumstances, both you and your child display the symptoms of co-dependent behavior because, along the way, you both have adapted to each other's dysfunctional behavior. In essence, the drug-abusing child and the co-dependent parent are both addictive personalities with symptoms that are linked and that work against each other's recovery. Moreover, both child and parent take on the persona of victim.

In the beginning, the drug-abusing child becomes increasingly focused on securing and using the drug she is dependent upon. The addiction dictates the child's lifestyle and quality of life. She learns to lie, if necessary, to protect her drug supply and freedom of use. With time, this way of life undermines the child's integrity and sense of values.

Such fundamental compromises eventually cause the child a high degree of discomfort, leading her to use drugs even more in an attempt to feel better about herself. One result: The chemical-dependent child develops a higher tolerance for the drug and must use more and more. Another result: The child's life undertakes a rapid decline.

For a while, the substance-abusing child denies that there is a problem, denies that her use of drugs is out of control. But now, when the drug itself no longer provides euphoric highs, the child needs to use drugs merely to feel "normal." At the same time, the co-dependent parent has begun to focus his life on the drug-abusing child, trying as hard to prevent the child from securing and using drugs as the child does to accomplish the opposite outcome. For example, parents often try to stop the child from hanging out with undesirable friends, or try to monitor the child's every movement. Sharon, the mother in the case study in Chapter One, provides a real-life example of how some parents attempt to exert tight control over their substance-abusing children when she tells of her all-night odysseys—with baseball bat in tow—to try to stop her son from selling cocaine.

In this type of situation, one parent frequently takes on the role of peacemaker in response to the havoc wrought by the activities of the child and the other controlling parent. The peacemaking parent, however, is also a co-dependent personality because he is still reacting to what is happening around him—adapting his behavior to take on the role of good guy rather than hanging tough, drawing a line, and seeking outside help.

Co-dependent parents will seek relief from the pain of this scenario. Defense techniques include the repression of emotions as well as a full-scale effort to become the calm and collected "superparent" who is able to handle anything and everything, particularly his child's addiction. Such tactics serve the same purpose as the adolescent's increasing abuse of drugs—just like the child, the co-dependent parent is trying to anesthetize emotional pain. And just like the substance-abusing child, the parent is eventually self-driven down a road of despair.

Co-dependency, in essence, is an unconscious game played by troubled families, families that have become dysfunctional. This game has its own set of destructive rules that are seldom overtly articulated but are routinely acted out. The rules are derived from unhealthy patterns of living practiced over a number of years. We learn them from our parents and pass them along. Ironically, these rules almost always originate from the parental desire to protect the family or from an individual family member's desire to psychologically protect himself.

Despite this gloomy scenario, there is a way out of this cycle. Parents can teach themselves and their children new rules, though this requires a significant effort and the courage to shoulder some of the responsibility for what is happening with family members. Ensuing chapters will give you guidance on the specifics of this process. For now, let's look at the "rules" that you, as a co-dependent parent, are probably following.

PLAYING BY THE RULES

As the above description demonstrates, the relationship between you and your chemically addicted child is complex and not easily encapsulated. Still, research reveals there are discernible though unspoken rules that dysfunctional, co-dependent families use to cope with life. Understanding the nature of these rules and their destructive impact on the family can be a big first step for parents who want to help their children overcome drugs and who want to help themselves overcome co-dependency. The next step is changing old behavioral patterns through the development of new rules that lead to a more healthy interaction between parents and their children.

Two leading substance-abuse experts in Minnesota, John Friel, director of Counseling Associates, and Robert Subby, executive director of Family Systems Center, explain the rules associated with co-dependency this way:

> Co-dependency . . . a dysfunctional pattern of living and problem-solving . . . is nurtured by a set of rules within the family system. These rules make healthy growth and change very difficult. . . . While change is almost always risky and scary, the benefits of learning new rules are well worth it: a clear sense of self, peace of mind, and comfortable relationships.

Essentially, the following rules represent ways of protecting or isolating family members from each other and from the outside world. Further, their underlying premise is that getting too close is too risky an undertaking.

RULE #1:
IT'S NOT OKAY
TO TALK ABOUT PROBLEMS

In some families, members are repeatedly admonished not to air the family's dirty linen in public. In other families, the message is just as strong though unspoken. In such families, parents and children never talk about problems, even to one another, despite the palpable tension. Adherence to this rule eventually causes family members to avoid their own problems. This rule allows co-dependent parents to pretend their substance-abusing children are healthy and doing well. It also permits such parents to absolve themselves from blame for their children's difficulties, since problems that are not discussed are not acknowledged to exist. Yet denying problems can foster a sense of impending doom.

Feeling that disaster may lie behind any door adds another layer of stress to an already stressful situation. Co-dependent parents who are still trying to pretend nothing is wrong with their substance-abusing child become powder kegs and thus render themselves impotent, in a way, from examining options that might lead to resolution of their family's problems. Parents who have managed to dull the impact of emotional feelings through long-term denial also dull their problem-solving ability.

RULE #2:
DO NOT EXPRESS FEELINGS OPENLY

In families with unresolved chemical and co-dependency issues, emotional blocking is commonly a serious problem. Parent and child alike may come to believe that it is better to deny feelings rather than to risk letting someone else see who they really are inside. Parents who teach their children ideas like "big boys don't cry" are providing examples of this rule. With time, this suppression of a child's emotional self becomes so complete that even he no longer knows who he really is.

My sister confirms that she suffered just this type of identity crisis shortly after my mother and father separated when she was close to 14. My father insisted that she play the role of surrogate mother for our younger brother and surrogate wife for him on an emotional level. He made it clear she was supposed to help him sort out the family's financial problems and schedule day-to-day routines such as grocery shopping and menu planning. If she complained, she was made to feel guilty. So she suppressed her feelings and turned to marijuana for escape.

RULE #3:
DON'T COMMUNICATE DIRECTLY;
USE ONE PERSON AS MESSENGER

My father was guilty of this process, called triangulation, after he and my mother were divorced. He needed money but was uncomfortable asking my mother directly to help him. Instead, he told me over and over how it would be nice if my mother would help him pay the mortgage. After a while I picked up on the fact that he wanted me to take this request to my mother. Speaking indirectly in this way can cause confusion, misdirected feelings, and dishonesty. Innocent family members become victims of the inability of others to confront personal problems directly. Speaking for my father nurtured my brand of co-dependency—I like to control people and manage their lives. In this instance, I got to control both of my parents in some measure, since Father used me as a messenger and since Mother accepted my role and didn't insist that my father speak for himself.

RULE #4:
HARBOR UNREALISTIC EXPECTATIONS
FOR THE CHILD

"Be strong, good, right, perfect. Make us proud." Co-dependent families tend to deliver the message that there is only one right way to achieve these goals. Moreover, the message of perfection is: Enough is never enough. These families create an ideal about what is good or right or best, and this ideal is so far removed from reality that parents and, particularly, children end up being nagged, pushed, and criticized for not living up to the family's expectations.

My sister, for example, says, "I never wanted to go to college. I just didn't give a damn about going, but I did it because I was expected to." By the time the first summer vacation approached, she recalls, she was smoking marijuana regularly. She lasted less than two years as a college student.

RULE #5: DON'T BE SELFISH

For the co-dependent parents who preside over a family system where this rule applies, feelings of guilt are certain to emerge. Such parents learn to view themselves as wrong for placing their own needs before the needs of others. What often happens in a family of co-dependents is that one of the members tries to feel good about himself by taking care of others to such a degree that his self-esteem actually becomes dependent on these caretaking or enabling activities. Without a substance-abusing child to take care of, the co-dependent parent is left with no purpose or worth. More than one family member may take on this role, further complicating the process.

RULE #6:
DO AS I SAY, NOT AS I DO

This rule, more than any other, teaches distrust. If, for example, co-dependent parents tell their child it's bad to be a substance abuser and then use drugs themselves, the child becomes confused and suspicious. Such children learn to count only on themselves out of a need to protect themselves from the pain of inconsistency. They may also rebel against their parents' dishonesty and do the very thing they have been instructed to avoid, such as using drugs. Indeed, many children who are in drug treatment centers have parents who are themselves recovering from a chemical or alcohol addiction.

Members of a co-dependent household also tend to suffer from externalization as a result of this "Do as I say, not as I do" rule. They become second-guessers who worry too much about doing only what they think others will want them to do. Second-guessing is an extremely unstable way to live that fosters high stress levels. High stress levels can lead to a child's feeling he needs to escape. That need to escape can lead to the use of drugs.

RULE #7:
IT'S NOT OKAY TO PLAY

To play is to risk being spontaneous, and perhaps even foolish, which is too scary for the co-dependent parent. From the very beginning, co-dependent parents believe that the world is a very serious place. Life is difficult and always painful. Consequently, the child who wants to play is imprisoned in the co-dependent family. Once again, suppression of healthy desires and emotions takes place. Emotional suppression, as pointed out before, can contribute to a child's feeling a strong need to escape from the confines of the family and perhaps turn to drugs.

Despite the pathological nature of co-dependent behavior suggested by these rules, parents who are helping their children overcome drugs should keep in mind the following words of hope: These rules can and should be broken. The following chapters discuss how to map out a new set of rules to live by. You can sort out the dynamics of co-dependency and its concomitant set of rules, and your family members can develop healthy relationships.

The following case study tracks a family in such a transition. Though still displaying co-dependent behavioral patterns, this family appears to be headed along a path of recovery.

CASE STUDY:
CHRISTY, RICHARD, AND JEREMY

Christy and Richard agree that their inability to communicate has hurt their only child, 17-year-old Jeremy. The admission, however, is one of the few areas about which they have reached an accord. Thirteen years ago the couple divorced and, according to Christy, 35, few kind words have passed between the two since, especially when the topic concerns their son. "There was a lot of animosity surrounding the divorce. Richard didn't want a divorce. Richard still hates the fact that I divorced him. But I left him because I wasn't happy with the way he chose to live his life, and I thought I could be happier without him." As it turns out, she adds, "I am happier."

Richard, 38, says that once a couple has had a child it isn't a "good plan" to divorce. "I think both parents should have an opportunity to provide equal input when a child is being raised. So I think that if a couple has had a child, they should stay together no matter what—the emphasis should be on the child." The couple married when Christy was 17 and Richard 20. Four years later they were divorced. What caused the demise of the relationship? "Honestly," Richard says, "I think we just got married way, way too young."

Christy, a resident of San Jose, California, has always had legal custody of Jeremy. Over the years she has allowed her son to spend a great deal of time living in Sacramento with his father, even though she reports that Richard "drinks a lot and smokes marijuana every day." Jeremy currently lives with his dad, who confesses that he used to drink a lot but now defines himself as a social drinker who partakes only on weekends when he partakes at all. Richard is the manager of a Mercedes-Benz service center. Christy designs printed circuit boards for an electronics company. Neither Richard nor Christy has remarried.

CHRISTY

Christy feels that her ex-husband has been a bad influence on Jeremy. "He used to buy cases of Jack Daniels and take Jeremy to go play war." "Playing war" meant that Richard, Jeremy, and some of Richard's friends would take shotguns to the backcountry and just shoot. They were arrested several times for their antics. "I wanted to share more subtle, more beautiful things about life with my son," Christy says, "and it was harder to share those things when he was being enticed to shoot guns."

It didn't take Jeremy long to figure out that he could use the conflict between his parents to manipulate them to get what he wanted. Once, for example, when his mother took Jeremy's skateboard from him as a form of punishment, he demanded to move back with his father if it wasn't returned. When the skateboard was not forthcoming, he called his father, who immediately drove 300 miles to pick him up. By the time he arrived, however, Jeremy had changed his mind.

Jeremy's substance-abuse problems began when he was 12, during a one-year period when he lived with his father. Christy can still recall vividly what happened. Richard's sister was a heroin addict with a son who was four years older than Jeremy. Because of his sister's problems,

Richard had agreed to let her son live with him. "This child was already in trouble," Christy says. "So when Jeremy moved in with his dad, everything started to head rapidly downhill. Jeremy stopped going to school so that he and his cousin could party all day long while Richard held a full-time job. At one point, Jeremy had a very, very terrible acid [LSD] experience that I didn't find out about until a month later."

According to Christy, Jeremy's father dropped him off for a brief visit with the terse comment, "Jeremy's having some emotional problems; you'd better look into it." She could tell something was really wrong. "Jeremy looked so frightened, I took a week off from work and took long walks with him. We talked a lot." During one of those talks Jeremy admitted he had tried LSD, and then he started to cry. "I was livid when I found out but decided there was nothing I could do about it—the damage had been done and couldn't be undone, so I didn't say much to Richard."

Jeremy eventually returned to live with his father where, Christy complains, he was permitted to run wild. "He had no limits. His father let him do anything. Then, I think, at some point Jeremy himself was afraid of how far his father might let him go." Shortly thereafter, his father announced that Jeremy was out of control and requested that Christy take over. For the next year or so she had a hard time dealing with Jeremy. There were problems at school and at home. But toward the end of that period things were beginning to improve, so she thought it was okay to take a month-long vacation to Africa. Jeremy remained at home under the supervision of one of Christy's friends, who had agreed to house-sit as well.

When Christy returned, she discovered that Richard had dropped off a runaway friend of Jeremy's to keep him company while Christy was gone and that neither child had been attending school. As best as Christy can determine, the boys had told her friend—whose duty it was to chaperone—a number of tall tales that she had accepted at face value. The freedom the boys gained from telling the lies had allowed them to use drugs, ditch school, and, generally, engage in mayhem. Christy blamed Richard for Jeremy's setback and decided to return him to his father. Christy told her ex-husband, "I really can't be effective unless I have your support. And since I don't, I can't deal with it, so let's do it your way. Jeremy should live with you."

Today, she admits, "I think that may have been a mistake." The time spent under his father's jurisdiction ended with Jeremy's expanding his drug use to include "crystal meth," or speed, and Jeremy started to steal to support his habit. He was only 16 by the time this occurred. Eventually he was arrested for possession of stolen property and for burglary. Jeremy was released from juvenile hall to attend Spring Creek Community, a boarding school in Thompson Falls, Montana, for troubled teenagers, including substance abusers. "At Spring Creek, we were taught that it's not just the child with a problem, it's the family that has a problem."

Christy believes that she tried harder than did her ex-husband and son to break the many patterns of dysfunctional behavior that continue to plague her family, such as Richard's tendency to come to Jeremy's rescue at the drop of a hat and her desire to want to "fix things" for Jeremy. "Richard," she says, "didn't cooperate with Jeremy's counselor at Spring Creek whatsoever." Further, she adds, "Jeremy didn't like his counselor because the counselor is a very strong figure. He's physically big and he's a no-nonsense type of person and he wouldn't let Jeremy get away with things—and Jeremy likes to get away with things."

She got the most out of the year Jeremy stayed at Spring Creek, she feels, because she made the biggest effort to participate in the group family sessions conducted there. Jeremy has been drug-free for about a year now. He currently lives with his father and works part-time for a fast-food operation. He attends school and is doing very well according to Christy, who hears from him by telephone once every week or two. Still, Christy has her doubts: "I have mixed feelings about how well Jeremy is doing, in part because I think he might be paying me lip service. But I do see some improvement, though I don't know how long this is going to last. So I am not very happy with the way this family has turned out. But I am happy with my life, and what I really want is for Jeremy to be happy with his life."

RICHARD

"It's real easy for a twelve-year-old to get drugs nowadays," Richard points out while explaining that Jeremy first started using marijuana by purchasing it from other children at school. "If a kid has five bucks, he can get just about any kind of drug he wants at his local high school. It's a real, drastic problem for parents to deal with right now."

Richard knew his son was using drugs because he recognized many of the signs. "All of a sudden Jeremy wanted to sleep in in the mornings. His attention span wasn't normal. And he didn't care about anything anymore. We tried to talk about what was going on, but it didn't work out. Soon he got way out of control, so I sent him back to his mother."

This pattern of Jeremy's moving back and forth between his mother and father during times of crisis continued for a few years, Richard acknowledges. As Jeremy grew older, however, his behavior grew worse. "Jeremy would just go away and stay with friends for four or five days at a time," Richard remembers. "It was past due for me to be an authority figure, but just before he finally ran away from me I saw that he refused to accept my authority."

It was during this period that Jeremy was arrested. "I thought the kid he was hanging out with was a kid. But later I found out the guy was twenty-three years old. I was shocked. He looked so young." It turns out that this man made a practice of preying on teenagers who had drug problems, getting them involved in burglary schemes to support their habits and to support himself. Explains Richard: "They got caught when they broke into my neighbor's house—only two doors down from me—in broad daylight with the neighbor at home. On April 13, 1987, that's when Jeremy went to juvenile hall."

By mid-June of that year, Jeremy was enrolled in Spring Creek. Richard likes some things about the school but does not like the "methods they use for therapy." He likes the school's Survival Course, which requires the children to hike as much as 100 miles over a three-week period and to manage with very little food. They are expected to live off the land. On the other hand, Richard does not like the way the parent group meetings are conducted. He feels that he's being pressured to not question the school and to become emotional. Richard is uncomfortable being put into either of those positions.

"These parent therapy sessions are very emotional. The counselor really tries to break a person down. It worked on Christy. After a while she did whatever the school said she should do about how to deal with Jeremy. Five years ago, she wouldn't have taken some of the positions she took with Jeremy." Still, Richard tried to go along with the program when Jeremy's counselor suggested the father "get some goals going for Jeremy." So, according to Richard, he and Jeremy made a deal: If Jeremy made excellent grades in the upcoming semester, he could go to Hawaii in the summer.

Inspired, Jeremy earned the grades, but he also broke the school's rules by putting two tattoos on the calf of his right leg: a skull with thorns sticking out and a skeleton of a bull that has big, ugly teeth. Richard recalls that his first thought was, "Why did Jeremy do this? Why wasn't he being supervised?" Jeremy's counselor suggested that the Hawaiian trip be cancelled. Christy agreed; Richard did not.

From Richard's point of view, his agreement to take Jeremy to Hawaii was based on the child's academic performance alone. As far as his grades went, Jeremy had done well, so Richard saw no need to renege on the trip. "I told Christy, 'There's no way I am going to tell Jeremy to his face that he can't go. There's no way I can turn my back on him. There's no way I can do that. It would make Jeremy feel so alone.'" Richard removed Jeremy from Spring Creek and they went to Hawaii.

Jeremy returned from the trip to live with his father. Within two days he got a job and has been saving to pay the insurance costs and repairs on an old car he has purchased. Because of the time he missed from school while using drugs, Jeremy's education is only at the tenth-grade level. Richard and Jeremy are looking into adult education programs that will allow Jeremy to attend school part-time, working toward a General Education Diploma (GED).

Jeremy has decided to become a lawyer. Richard also proudly relates that his drug-free son "gets on me about smoking cigarettes."

JEREMY

"I took drugs because I had so much fun doing it. But when you come down [after using drugs] you don't feel good, so you use drugs to feel better," 17-year-old Jeremy points out. "I was around eleven years old when I first started using drugs. I didn't think about it too much because everybody I hung around with used drugs." Jeremy started smoking marijuana after coming to live with his father and a 16-year-old cousin. It was this cousin who introduced Jeremy to drugs.

By the time he was 13, Jeremy says, "I was doing all kinds of drugs—LSD, opium, and mushrooms. My dad knew I was using drugs by the time I was in the eighth grade, but at first he didn't think that there was any problem with it." When asked why he was so sure his father knew what was going on, Jeremy explains, "He knew after a while because we talked about it." During this period Jeremy returned to live with his mother.

"Then she went on vacation to Africa right when one of my friends had been kicked out by his parents. He was fourteen years old and had no place to go, so I let him stay with me. He slept in the garage, and the lady who was supposed to be looking after me while my mother was gone never knew that my friend was really living in the garage. When my mother came back she found out right away. She called my dad and said she didn't even want me back. So I lived with my dad, and by then I was out of control."

He used methamphetamine regularly. "It keeps you

awake. I would stay up for three or four days at a time and then come home and sleep for hours and hours." Jeremy admits that he broke into houses and into cars to support his drug habit. He also sold stolen marijuana. "People in this part of California grow a lot of marijuana plants during the summer. You can smell where they're growing, so we would just sneak over fences and steal enough of the plant to sell a pound or more at a time. We made a lot of money." A pound of stolen marijuana plants would sell for $1,600, "give or take $200." Jeremy was 14 at the time.

Soon Jeremy was arrested for burglary. "My dad got me out and they let me off, but between two weeks and a month later I got caught with stolen merchandise. The stuff was in my garage. I was put in juvenile hall for two months." Eventually he was released to attend Spring Creek Community.

Jeremy thinks that the school was especially tough. "They [Spring Creek counselors] play a lot of head games. They say things like, 'We have total control over you.' 'You're not going to get out of here until you deal with your parents.'" He describes the specific counselor assigned to him as "cold-blooded and ruthless. Seriously, I didn't trust him. Once he picked me and two friends up and told us we were going skiing. Then he drove us to the middle of nowhere and we had to hike for four days. We ate one meal a day—a bowl of rice—and slept in sleeping bags without tents in seventeen-degree weather."

To defy authority, Jeremy says, he tattooed himself. "I just decided that it was something that I could do that they couldn't do anything about." At the time, Jeremy says, he didn't like anything about Spring Creek. Now, he acknowledges, "What I think I got out of it was it kept me sober long enough to think about what I was doing with my life." Jeremy left Spring Creek in August 1988. Currently he lives with his father in Sacramento. He calls his mother regularly and believes his life has taken a definite turn for the better.

"Things are a lot easier now. I don't have to worry about everything. When I see a sheriff, I don't have to worry. And now that I'm sober, I can think about what I want my life to be like and try to make the best happen. I'm going to AA [Alcoholics Anonymous] meetings two or three times a week. It keeps me thinking right. After I finish high school I want to go to college and then law school." Asked if it is hard for him to stay away from drugs, Jeremy says, "Once you're on the path it's easy not to use drugs. It's harder to get on the path."

POSTSCRIPT

"Jeremy is a chronically dependent young man," reports his former counselor at Spring Creek, who asked to go unnamed. "By his own reports Jeremy used methamphetamine, marijuana, and alcohol. He's a polydrug user." Jeremy's history was that he would stay with his mother until he was bored, then would go live with his father. But, the counselor notes, "whenever criminality took place, the father, in frustration and unknowingness, would call the mother and say, 'I don't know what to do—take over.'

"Richard doesn't want to be the 'bad guy'; that's his terminology," the counselor adds. As proof he cites the way Jeremy addressed his parents in letters. "Jeremy referred to his father in correspondence as 'Yo Dude.' Letters to his mother had a very different and more respectful tone." On the other hand, the counselor surmised that Christy's difficulty with co-dependence had to do with some unresolved feelings and anger around her divorce. "It's impossible for her to take a bottom-line stand with Richard. Though in the last meeting before Richard removed Jeremy from the school she did get tough," the counselor recalls.

"Richard," he says, "is a very pleasant person over the phone. He appears to be compassionate. But in person he demonstrates something else. His conflict style is passive-aggressive." One example the counselor gives involves an evening when Richard drove to the school and picked Jeremy up without saying anything to anybody. He returned Jeremy seven days later, in the middle of the night. Richard tended to avoid face-to-face meetings with Spring Creek staff, the counselor notes, so he didn't take part in many of the parent group meetings. Christy did take part, "in a very independent and healthy way."

"Jeremy was looking at one year solid incarceration time when the Spring Creek intervention took place," the counselor says. At Spring Creek, Jeremy bonded with the subgroups, or children on the fringes of "punk" culture. Still, the counselor reports, "Jeremy was quite a playful and pleasant person to be around when engaged in sports activities. But when confronted with task completion he became sullen and withdrawn."

The counselor has a somewhat different point of view than Richard of the Hawaiian vacation that led to Jeremy's departure from Spring Creek. "In some way I take exception that Richard took Jeremy away, because that action implies that he [Jeremy] was faced with some evil presence. The entire counseling treatment team recommended that Jeremy not go to Hawaii but that Richard and Jeremy spend time together on the campus. We asked him [Richard], 'Do you want to reinforce Jeremy's negative behavior by rewarding him with a vacation?' Richard said no, but by the time he arrived to see Jeremy, he had changed his mind."

Jeremy had a tattoo on his hand before arriving at Spring Creek. During his tenure at the school, the counselor says, Jeremy made a tattoo gun and placed additional tattoos on himself and other students.

The counselor forecasts a fairly circumscribed future for Jeremy unless he receives long-term treatment. "I think Jeremy's problem with intimacy will plague him for quite some time. He has difficulty with trust, with boundaries. I think Jeremy will suffer from episodic relapses that will result in incarceration unless professional treatment is sought and both he and his father abide by that advice."

Both Christy and Richard express regrets about their roles in Jeremy's downfall. "When he was so terribly strung out on acid," Christy recalls, "he was like a blank canvas. I remember thinking that at the time. When a person's in that condition you can do almost anything with him to direct him in the right direction. Boy, I wish I had done something then." But, she says, she returned him to his father because "I didn't want to rescue Jeremy. That's one of his problems." Christy feels that if she had been stronger and could have afforded to send him to a boarding school sooner, she might have been able to help Jeremy. However, she laments, "The money [from having increased her income over the years] came too late."

Richard feels he failed Jeremy by not showing his son "where the buck stops. Just doing that would have been the most important thing for Jeremy. Parents are the only real guidance children have. But I didn't like being a disciplinarian." Things appear to be different now. As Richard describes it, he and Jeremy "have a talk once a week where we both get to say whatever is bothering us. Jeremy also is required, every night, to make a list of whatever he plans to do the next day. Jeremy thinks it's a 'retarded idea,' but it's one of my new rules, and it's something he has to live with."

Clearly, Christy and Richard displayed co-dependent behavior by playing into Jeremy's manipulations and thus enabling him to use drugs and miss school. But is Richard's concern over not having drawn a stricter line with Jeremy a reasonable concern? Did the strict lines Christy drew help or hurt Jeremy? Such questions are examined in the following chapter, "Hanging Tough."

❧ 3 ❧

Hanging Tough

Hanging tough may be the right thing to do when dealing with a drug-dependent family member, but it certainly is not the easy thing to do. I learned this lesson a few years ago when my cocaine-addicted sister came to live with me. Hanging tough involved giving up my co-dependent desire to rescue her, and it also involved drawing a line, establishing boundaries beyond which I would not allow her to cross. To do so was particularly difficult for me because I felt as if I was being selfish. What I didn't know then but have since come to understand is that being selfish under such circumstances is okay.

For years I had carried around a powerful image of my sister: She was my live paper doll. As a child she had been very cute, very smart, and quite personable. I found pleasure in buying her beautiful clothes and jewelry during her adolescent years. So when she arrived on my doorstep in her mid-twenties bedraggled and in need of financial and emotional support, I was quick to come to the rescue. In retrospect, her drug problem should have been easy to spot. But at first I simply could not come to grips with the new image of the young woman who stood before me.

As my sister's behavior deteriorated and I finally had

to face the fact that she was addicted to rock cocaine, another complication arose that prevented me from taking swift and decisive action against her: I found out she was pregnant, intended to keep the child, and was not necessarily going to get married. I remember saying over and over again in conversations with my best friend, "How can I put my pregnant sister out into the streets?"

Though my sister remained employed up until her sixth month of pregnancy, she could account for less and less of her money as her cocaine addiction grew worse. Toward the end of her tenure at my home she no longer set aside money for food or transportation to and from her job. Instead, she relied on me, other family members, and friends to meet her most basic needs. And for a long time we all came through for her. After all, how could anyone let an unmarried, pregnant woman starve?

Despite warnings from my friends that for my own good I had to ask my sister to leave, I continued to try to "help" and she continued to use drugs. Eventually, the situation peaked when I discovered that my sister had made many more long-distance calls on my telephone than she could afford, and that a drug dealer had begun to visit my household regularly. I banned the dope peddler from my home, was stuck with an expensive telephone bill, and faced a tough decision I could not escape: Her pregnancy notwithstanding, my sister had to go.

Hanging tough for me was watching my sister leave, knowing that she had burned her bridges and had nowhere to go. She ended up spending some time in a shelter for the homeless before she finally gave up cocaine and had a healthy child. It was a long time before I could leave my guilt behind and believe that my choice had been the right one.

My guilt and pain reemerged a year later, when my

sister found out I was working on this book and we sat down to talk about what had happened during those troublesome days. What I found out was that I had failed her in some significant way by drawing the line so late in the game. Just as she had wanted my father to tell her no, she had wanted me to tell her to stop using drugs:

> Dad could have asked some very pointed questions, he could have followed me, but he didn't and I know why he didn't: Dad was too wrapped up in his own problems. He was worrying about his marriage coming to an end. So the most he did for me was the obligatory things to do, but his heart wasn't in it. He never asked that I leave a phone number of where I was going to be, for example. And if he wasn't going to ask any questions, I wasn't going to volunteer any information. Since I was only fourteen or fifteen years old, I took advantage of the situation, though I don't know too many fourteen- or fifteen-year-olds who wouldn't have.

It was hard for me to hear my sister's depiction of what had happened with my father, because she hit too close to home. I, too, had neglected to ask my sister the necessary "pointed questions." Over and over again my sister has told me in our recent discussions that she had wanted my help, she had wanted me to ask her why she was doing these things to herself. She still doesn't quite understand what took me so long to decide to hang tough.

SETTING PRIORITIES: FIRST THINGS FIRST

I tend to disagree with my sister's beliefs about why our father chose to remain quiet while she abused drugs, based on my own reactions to her drug problem. I didn't move as fast as I could have because I was scared that to draw a line would indicate a lack of tolerance and, thus, a lack of love on my part. Understanding what I understand now, as well as no longer being in the middle of the fray, I can see more clearly that such a point of view was yet another reflection of my co-dependent behavior. By caring about what cutting my sister off might "indicate" to others, I was really serving as my sister's enabler: I was more concerned about my own image than in helping her overcome drugs.

These days, I also recognize that my co-dependency involved playing the martyr's role. As long as my sister stuck around and abused my hospitality, I could feel superior by showing that I could handle the worst of situations with strength and perseverance. I have since learned that hanging tough—accepting the legitimacy of the boundaries I set, acknowledging that some behavior is intolerable indeed—was the appropriate thing to do, for my sister and for myself.

Admittedly, hanging tough—through setting the priority that you must take care of yourself first—is a scary and guilt-provoking step for many parents. I worried many nights over how my sister was faring. And I have certainly spent many nights lamenting my co-dependent behavior that, in some ways, nurtured my sister's chemical dependency by postponing her inevitable fall. Having experienced what I experienced, it's easy for me to relate to why Richard, the father in Chapter Two's case study, allowed his son to run rampant for so long before seeking outside help. In light of what has happened, his ex-wife's tendency to regret her more hard-line approach—to insist that her son make his own decisions and, thus, not intervene—is also not too difficult to understand.

According to Steven W. Cawdrey, headmaster and co-founder of Montana's Spring Creek Community, "Traditionally we've been raised to believe that selfishness is self-centeredness. Self-centeredness is dysfunctional and a characteristic of co-dependency; selfishness is not." Cawdrey points out that it is healthy to say to your substance-abusing child, "I will not be treated this way; I don't deserve it." Interestingly enough, by taking such actions and thus taking care of yourself first, you are also helping your troubled child. "Addictive personalities have to get other people and institutions to buy into their behavior in order to actively engage in co-dependency," Cawdrey notes. Setting clear boundaries, then, is the appropriate way to deal with your child who is using drugs. "If you create boundaries, a person has to face himself in the mirror. Always, always, always, a diseased person should be faced with what you are observing about his behavior and asked to make a choice to either change or continue practicing the disease."

So, as difficult as it might be, parents who help their children overcome drugs have to learn how to hang tough, to set priorities, and be prepared to handle their own symptoms of co-dependency such as their need to rescue, to enable, to believe that it's not okay to take care of themselves first. On my own, I eventually sought the services of a psychologist. Most reputable drug-treatment programs include counseling for all members of the family on an individual and group basis. Some programs virtually require that at least one parent get involved in the treatment program.

Cawdrey advises the parents of addicted children who attend his residential facility to prioritize their efforts to maintain themselves and their family in the following way:

1. Work on Stabilizing Your Relationship with Yourself

What are your needs? What are your limits? What do you understand and what don't you understand about what's going on? Make sure you can honestly answer such questions.

2. Work on Stabilizing Your Relationship with Your Spouse or Significant Other

Are you ignoring your spouse in order to deal with problems caused by your child's drug abuse? What about the family's finances? Has your spouse had to sacrifice a long-saved-for purchase to pay the legal fees of your troubled child?

3. Work on Stabilizing the Lives of the Other Members of the Family Unit, Including Siblings as Well as the Young Substance Abuser

Have you noticed whether a sister or brother who is not on drugs is having problems with schoolwork? Is the sibling who shares a bedroom with the substance-abusing child being pressured as well to use drugs? Is the troubled child stealing from the sibling?

4. Take Care That You Don't Harm Your Relationships with People at Your Workplace by Your Reaction to Familial Stresses

Are you arguing with your co-workers more frequently than ever before? Is your work product showing signs of deterioration? Have you become unreliable or unpredictable so that your subordinates or superiors are beginning to complain to you and to others?

EASIER SAID THAN DONE—
BUT WORTH THE TROUBLE

As simple as this prescription for recovery is, it is not always easy to follow. Parents typically find it hard to put themselves first when their substance-abusing child consistently maneuvers to be rescued from potentially critical situations—and not-so-critical situations. Jeremy, the teenager discussed in the last chapter's case study, provides a prime example.

As you'll recall, when his mother, Christy, took away his skateboard to punish him for some inappropriate deed, he called his father to come and get him. Richard dropped what he was doing and drove for three hours to pick up his son—without calling Christy to clarify Jeremy's claims—only to find that Jeremy had changed his mind by the time his father arrived.

Richard felt that "hanging tough"—to stay put and let Jeremy deal with his problem on his own—would have been less than helpful to his son. He believed that coming to Jeremy's rescue was the proper thing to do. Richard's co-dependent behavior involved a need to be a "buddy" to Jeremy rather than an authority figure. Ironically, however, the message Jeremy received from his father's rescuing actions undermined his confidence in himself. It was a message that said, "You can't deal with your own problems. You're incompetent. You're weak." By consistently hanging tough, on the other hand, Richard would have encouraged Jeremy to face the direct consequences of his actions. In dealing with unpleasant situations on his own, Jeremy would have developed the experience and maturity that lead to feelings of self-confidence and pride.

Hanging tough with a drug-abusing child, and thus giving your own needs first consideration, poses special problems in dealing with a spouse. The other parent may not yet recognize the wisdom of refusing to rescue an addicted child and will continue to do so, even when experience has demonstrated that rescuing does not help. Some parents have gone so far as to financially and emotionally bankrupt the family in order to "save" the addicted adolescent.

While Cawdrey's four-pronged guidelines for parents who are trying to help their children overcome drugs may not be easy to follow, for those parents who accept the challenge, there is hope in knowing that these guidelines can produce successful results. Adhering to these guidelines can also serve as a basis for helping parents to rewrite the rules of co-dependency outlined in Chapter Two:

Rule #1: It's not okay to talk about problems.

Rule #2: Do not express feelings openly.

Rule #3: Don't communicate directly; use one person as messenger.

Rule #4: Harbor unrealistic expectations for the child.

Rule #5: Don't be selfish.

Rule #6: Do as I say, not as I do.

Rule #7: It's not okay to play.

Taking a hanging-tough approach to dealing with your child requires revision of the first three rules in order to create boundaries, to draw lines. As a parent who is hanging tough, you must confront your substance-abusing child with the behavioral problems you have observed. This process requires you to express your feelings of distress openly and directly to your child. Moreover, unrealistic expectations for your child (Rule #4) have no place in the hanging-tough scenario. What's at issue is the choice your child is prepared to take, *on her own,* between abusing drugs and living a full life. As described by Cawdrey, "Children who use drugs need to be forced to make one of two conscious decisions: either (1) they continue to practice using drugs, which is choosing to die, or (2) they are willing to ask for help, which is choosing to live." Expecting your child to opt for one of these choices is not unrealistic.

As for Rule #5, remember, hanging tough means that you understand the benefits to yourself and to your substance-abusing child of looking out for number one first. Rule #6 is inoperable when a parent is attempting to hang tough; such hypocrisy and dishonesty are the antithesis of a hanging-tough approach. When you draw lines and establish boundaries you are, by definition, letting your child know precisely what you will and will not tolerate. You are insisting that neither you nor your child will cut any corners. Your message is not ambiguous, as is the case with a parent who is laboring under the "Do as I say, not as I do" mode of behavior.

The last rule involves the suppression of emotions. Again, this rule violates the basic premise of hanging tough. As a parent, you need to let your child know what you are feeling and, in addition, you want your child to communicate in an equally straightforward way what is on her mind and what is in her heart.

The next chapter will introduce a concept called "raising the bottom," the second phase of the hanging-tough concept. It explains how establishing an intervention method can cause your child to feel as if she has hit rock bottom although, in truth, a safety net is in place. For now, however, Eve and Mickey's story provides another opportunity to see how hanging-tough can be put to work. Every family is different, so don't expect neat and clean solutions—results of that kind are simply unrealistic.

This family has two adolescent sons who have used drugs and two daughters who have not. The youngest son refused to be interviewed for this book. He recently ran away from boarding school and currently lives outside the home. His parents believe he is still using drugs. The oldest son, who has since recovered enough from his use of drugs to attend college, agreed to share his experiences. The father declined to allow the daughters to participate in this project. Much of Frank's tale (the son who refused to participate) is told by his mother, Eve, and by his stepbrother, Mike.

CASE STUDY:
EVE, MICKEY, MIKE, AND FRANK

When Eve and Mickey married nine years ago, it was the second time around for both. Each brought children to the newly established family, so they expected some complications. What they eventually had to cope with, however, is quite another matter. Mike, Mickey's 19-year-old son, began using drugs and basically kept the house in an uproar, according to both Eve and Mickey. "When I came home I never knew what was going to hit me in the face," Mickey says. Eve's son, Frank, 17, also contributed to the family disorder by lying, stealing, and abusing drugs.

The activities of Mike and Frank "threatened the new marriage," Mickey reports. The boys' behavior also affected the couple's two younger children: Laurie, 13, Eve's daughter from her former marriage and Frank's sister; and 16-year-old Amy, Mickey's daughter and Mike's sister. "Laurie does not trust males," states Eve, "and Amy feels the great loss of never having had a real relationship with her brother." The family lives in a large home in a suburb of Charlotte, North Carolina. Eve, 40, is a housewife, though she worked earlier in the marriage; Mickey, 46, is a real estate appraiser.

EVE

Frank's problems started to show up in the sixth grade, Eve recalls, when he was living with her ex-husband, who had remarried. "Frank was signing his stepmother's name to report cards and school papers. He was stealing from both households—his father's and mine. And Frank would lie a lot, but if later he was caught he would say that you had misunderstood what he had said." In addition, Eve says, "Earlier on Frank had acted out sexually with his sister and younger brother [from his father's second marriage]."

Frank came to live with Eve and Mickey in June of 1986 because his stepmother had had two miscarriages, which she felt were brought on by the stress of having to deal with Frank. Eve agreed to the move because Frank conned her into believing that he was being treated unfairly at his father's home. "I accepted his story hook, line, and sinker. But what Frank really wanted was a more liberal household. I'm more open than his father, who's an extreme disciplinarian and who doesn't believe in therapy."

Two weeks after he arrived at her home, Frank was caught with marijuana. "In my household there are no cigarettes even, because I'm allergic to smoke. So when I smelled the pot Frank had been smoking, I knew that something was going on. I searched his room and found the proof of what I was suspecting. When I confronted Frank, he tried to lie to get out of trouble, but, of course, we knew he wasn't telling the truth." As it turned out, Frank's use of marijuana was only the beginning of many behavioral problems.

"Frank took a fire extinguisher and sprayed it inside the sanctuary of the church," Eve recalls. He also "rocked a car" (threw rocks at a vehicle) because "he thought it would be a fun thing to do," Eve says with some exasperation. "He was acting out sexually with a lot of girls, including a girl who was twelve and the daughter of an FBI agent. Frank was fifteen at the time. He would steal my car at night to go out with the girl. The girl's father was threatening to bring charges against Frank, but that didn't seem to faze Frank one bit. He continued to sneak around with the girl."

Frank stole money from Eve that she assumed she had spent, and by tenth grade he was cutting school more than he was attending classes. But at home, Eve remembers, "Frank was personable and easy to get along with, if you could accept that he rarely told the truth. Frank's the kind of person who can steal from you but you still love him to death." During this period Frank graduated in his drug use to taking speed, LSD, and, Eve and Mickey suspected, cocaine. Eve sought outside help from a therapist and discovered that Frank has a borderline personality disorder that she describes this way: "He's stuck in doing things that show intense rebellion. He refuses to accept that he cannot get anything that he wants at whatever price he has to pay, or whatever price someone else has to pay."

After repeated warnings from the FBI agent about his affair with the 12-year-old daughter, Frank scooped the girl up one night and the two of them helped another adolescent girl run away, broke into a house, and bought $100 worth of marijuana from Mike.

Ordinarily, Eve says, her co-dependent pattern of behavior would have set in. "I don't like fighting with the kids. When there are problems, I try to explain away the issue at hand, I try to make everything right. I make excuses for the children, I keep them from paying the price that they should." This time, however, Eve and Mickey decided to hang tough, to act in a unified manner to confront the problem and connect Frank with the consequences of his actions.

"When Frank got caught, he looked at his situation as if he were an outsider," Eve says. "He wasn't upset about what might happen to him. He wasn't afraid of going to jail." Frank was sent away to Spring Creek Community in Montana, a boarding school that specializes in dealing with children who have emotional difficulties and who are drug abusers.

His exploits continued. "At the boarding school, Frank and some friends managed to swim the river near the school and then walk five miles to the nearest town to steal cigarettes, which he wrapped in plastic so that they wouldn't get soaked when he swam back across the river." Frank also tattooed himself extensively and learned how to use nutmeg to get high. "He would mix water with nutmeg and then drink it to get a flash high that lasts for about two minutes. He also smelled fumes to get high, and before he ran away from the school he dug out a smoking room under one of the cabins. The room was big enough to hold two and three people, and when it wasn't in use, that's where the booty [cigarettes] was stored." As described by Eve, "Frank is a high energy mover-and-shaker who will either end up president of the United States or the godfather in the Mafia. He's that type of person; he's got that type of drive."

Eve contrasts Frank with Mickey's son, Mike, introverted, quiet, reserved, yet who kept the house in an uproar in his own way. "He did so very passively through a hundred small actions a day. He would leave crumbs on the table and if you asked him to clean up behind himself he would say, 'No. I'm not going to do that,' and sit down. Or he might come in late and turn on the light that he knew would shine into our bedroom. If asked about it he would say, 'Why don't you close your door?'"

"Mike's personality and mine are the opposite," Eve adds. "He's very self-centered. He does for himself only, although everything he does sounds logical to me but feels rotten." Up until Mike was about eight or nine he lived with his mother, who, Eve says, "taught the kids that the only thing you have to worry about in life is taking care of yourself."

When Mike was about 13, he went away to camp as a junior counselor and began to experiment with marijuana. When he returned he shared this experience with Eve and Mickey. "We told him that he should wait to experiment with drugs until he was older and in a more safe place. We told him that camp definitely was not a safe place and that using drugs was not a safe thing to do now." He didn't listen, and by the time he was 16, Mike was enrolled in the same boarding school that Frank eventually attended.

Eve and Mickey made the decision to send Mike to Spring Creek after his behavior became disruptive to the entire family. It took a lot of discomfort on everyone's part to draw such a rigid line, but by all accounts the decision has paid off for the entire family. "Mike ended up being the valedictorian when he graduated from Spring Creek. He now has self-confidence and he's learned how to motivate people. And what we really feel good about is Mike's acknowledgment of us. He toasted his dad and me for sending him to Spring Creek and for seeing what he needed even when he didn't know what he needed," Eve explains.

Eve is also pleased with the effect family counseling has had on her own personality, her marriage, and her relationship with the rest of the family. "I am less controlling and more willing to let people live their own lives nowadays. I am more willing to let my family see my hurt, not just my anger." In addition, Eve is excited about the progress her family has made. "The process that we have been going through has taken what was two family groups and made them into one. We are much more effective now. The kids get more of what they want, if it's appropriate, and we get more of what we want. Plus, my marriage is a whole lot better than it used to be, because we know now why we do what we do."

MICKEY

"Both of the boys have had general behavior problems. Mike couldn't relate to the family and to friends. He was very disruptive. Frank has had some problems with honesty and has been in trouble with the police," says Mickey, a pleasant man who repeatedly stated that Eve would be a better person to talk to about topics of this nature. "I think she can give you more of the emotional side of this than I." Still, Mickey was willing to offer his own theory about the source of Mike's problem. "Mike never quite coped with my divorce from his mother, Sarah. In fact, he saw a psychologist off and on for about seven or eight years before attending Spring Creek at the age of seventeen."

Moreover, when Mickey married Eve, Mike had trouble making the adjustment, although "Eve has been an excellent mother to the kids." Eventually Mike started using marijuana, and though shy and reserved outside the home, he was argumentative and aggressive among immediate family members. Explains Mickey: "There were a lot of arguments and fights and screaming matches provoked by Mike. Our family stayed in a constant uproar. We tried everything to help Mike, but he was on a dead-end street. Something had to change."

Mike was sent to Spring Creek and remained there for a couple of years. "They sent me back a new and improved kid, so I can't kick about that," Mickey says. Mike is currently enrolled in his first year of college. Frank, on the other hand, recently ran away from Spring Creek. He has lived with his grandparents in Savannah, Georgia, and with his birth father in Charlotte, North Carolina. Eve and Mickey will not allow him to return to their household. "Frank had had problems for years. He has used cocaine and LSD and got into trouble with the police. He would slip out at night and steal the family car. We would hide the keys, but he would steal the car anyway. Basically, we couldn't control him."

From time to time, Mickey thinks about how he could have done more for the children. "I didn't spend enough time with the kids; I pretty much had my plate full." He says that the counseling he received while trying to assist the boys has helped him overcome his longstanding, codependent habit of feeling guilty about the past. "I've pretty well worked through my guilt problem, but the family isn't perfect. Kids can manipulate the hell out of you. Kids really know where the buttons can be pushed," he says with a chuckle.

MIKE

Mike, now concentrating on math in college, says he will probably become a psychology major because he wants to help people, as he has been helped. His own problems began a number of years ago, though the escalation was gradual. "I guess from junior high on it just kinda got worse and worse. It wasn't a real drastic thing at all. Throughout much of the time I was fighting with my parents a lot. I totally did not get along with my family. I had like very little motivation for school. So I was getting poor grades and I was very angry. The bottom line was I had no confidence in myself.

"I fought with my parents all the time about typical teenage things, like clothes and grades and who I could see and all that stuff, except that it was really bad. I hated them. Then the summer before the tenth grade I started drinking a lot, and later on I started smoking pot to see what it was like. But then I was so unhappy with my life I started doing that like every day."

Mike used his allowance from mowing the lawn and income from a summer job to support his marijuana habit. He never used any other drugs; "I just did a lot of marijuana." Eventually his parents figured out that Mike was involved in some type of substance abuse as he began to return home from late Saturday night outings "messed up. So they knew I had done it [used drugs] a couple of times, but they weren't aware of the extent I was doing it. And every time I did it they would punish me or something, but I still did it anyway." Using drugs, Mike admits in hindsight, was a crutch he used to escape from life, to seclude himself.

Toward the end of his junior year in high school, Mike recalls, "Every night I would be screaming at my dad or Eve would be screaming at me. My house was like a battleground. I just can't explain how bad it was. I hated my life. I had very few friends. All I really cared about was getting stoned. I knew my life was pretty miserable. My parents were thinking, 'He's doing pretty bad in school, so we want to get him to a school that will turn his life around so that he will be happy.' I kinda agreed because my life was pretty miserable, plus I wanted to get away from my parents. I also agreed because I was too afraid to run away. I had nowhere else to go."

Meanwhile, about the time Mike started using pot, Frank started as well, although Mike didn't know it. "At first I didn't want Frank to know what I was doing because I didn't want to be a bad example. But then when we found out about each other we started getting high together. So we covered up for each other, we shared our drugs together, we did all of the same stuff, except he was kind of worse. He broke into houses and stole money and I never got into that. I was very careful about not getting kicked out of the house or whatever. Frank just didn't really care what happened."

Eve and Mickey brought up the issue of sending Mike to Spring Creek in the middle of his junior year. He knew for several months that his parents were looking for schools that might help him. "Every week they would tell me what schools they were looking at, and when they decided on Spring Creek they took me to see the educational consultant they had been working with, who explained the school to me. So I had a pretty good idea about what was going on."

Throughout this period Mike was getting further and further behind in his studies, but "I never skipped school. I went to school every day, but I never studied. I had like straight D's. I got F's all the time. I was at the bottom of my class, because all I cared about was getting high. I would go to school and sleep in class and walk around and sort of drift through life. It was pretty hopeless."

Once Mike landed at Spring Creek, everything opened up for him. "I liked Spring Creek. Most people really hate being there because you can't eat red meat and there's no television and you can't smoke. Most people hate it because of that type of stuff. Plus they're away from their friends and everything. But I liked it because for one of the first times in my life I was accepted for who I was. I started to feel better about myself and I felt confident enough to do things that I was afraid of before, like making friends, taking leadership roles in the school, stuff like that."

Toward the end of his two years at Spring Creek, Mike became the head of the honor society. "I had a lot of respect there. Before at my old school I talked to about two guys and no one knew me and no girls really liked me or anything. So it just felt pretty good. It's kinda like I got to start all over." When asked what was so different between the Mike who attended school in North Carolina and the Mike who was enrolled at Spring Creek, he offers the following observation:

"It was partly me and partly the school. I'm not really sure how this happened, but I just started off feeling comfortable to be open, to let people get to know me. I felt confident enough to just be myself, whereas at the other school I was so shy and insecure that I avoided people. I was so afraid that people would hate me, I didn't really try to get to know anyone. Plus at Spring Creek the students are a lot more accepting, because people are honest there and real and they care a lot about how you feel compared to your average school. People there are a lot more accepting, also."

Despite Mike's success at this school, a few of his actions were less than exemplary during his first six-month tenure. "I managed to sneak in some pot several times. The one big occasion that happened was when I went home for my first vacation. Even though I was doing pretty good at Spring Creek, I still had this big craving to get high. So I went home and smoked pot and I brought some back to the school and they found it. I got in trouble for that—I had to work at a mentally retarded center for a week. I actually liked my punishment, but it was my consequence. Then I got caught [again] about a month later."

This time Mike says that his "consequence" was a bit more difficult to cope with. "They have these things called compacts, where they put you out into the woods for a week with one staff member and depending on what time of the year it is, they work you. And since it was in February, I was cross-country skiing every day and sleeping in the woods and it was really hard."

Mike secured the marijuana that was responsible for his weeklong punishment at a racquetball club. He says that "some guy just gave it to me." He admits, with a laugh, that in those days he was "real open to finding it. I kinda kept my eye out, I suppose." That was the last time Mike has smoked marijuana—approximately 18 months ago as of the date of this interview. He does drink beer occasionally, he says, "but it's just college stuff."

Seven months after Mike arrived at Spring Creek, his stepbrother, Frank, joined him. "I was really looking forward to his coming, because we were pretty close. But when he got there it was different, because when we were friends in North Carolina we were like beer buddies, covering up our drugs and everything. But when he got to Spring Creek, we didn't *not* get along, we just didn't talk. We were pretty distant. We just never hung out. And, now, we get along okay but we're just very different people with very different goals in life, so we never really talk."

From Mike's point of view he and Frank differ in some significant ways. "I made it out of adolescence in one piece. . . . I've got some definite goals in life and some pretty strong values about what's right and wrong. As far as a career, I want to either be a therapist, some sort of social helping career, or I want to be an architect. I'm not really sure. I don't want to judge Frank or anything, but he just has this what-the-hell attitude about life. He doesn't seem to care about anything. He sort of has no sense of conscience at all about what's right or wrong. One time, for example, at Spring Creek he broke into the nurse's house and took her alcohol. It was like this big thing and he said he was sorry and he got punished for it, but then a week later he did the same thing to the same nurse. He just doesn't seem to have any idea of morality. He does stuff that it's so obvious that he's going to get caught, but he still does it. I don't understand where he's coming from." When asked if he thinks he can help Frank, Mike replies, "No. I don't know if anyone can."

In terms of his relationships with his younger sisters, Mike explains, "What I had done before Spring Creek was really isolate myself. I stayed in my room much of the time. I got along with them okay, I didn't really fight with them—well, sometimes I did, but they were in such a different world that I just didn't interact with them that much."

Mike says that he can "talk for years" about what he

got out of Spring Creek. During this interview, he manages to provide an abbreviated list of his gains. "I feel a lot better about myself—that's basically the biggest thing. I have a lot more confidence in myself and I know what I need to do to get what I want in life." So what does he need to do? "That's a big question. I just need to keep my goals straight and I need to discipline myself to go to classes. As far as emotionally, when I get depressed and stuff, I need to take care of myself and not just bottle up my feelings and I need to talk to someone and to remind myself that I'm still an okay person."

Mike says that his first month of college has truly tested the skills he learned at Spring Creek. "At Spring Creek, everyone is very honest with their feelings, very vulnerable. You can cry in front of thirty people and it's okay. But in college the guys are all macho and I really do not get into that at all. And it's been kinda hard because people are just really shallow. A lot of people are not willing to expose who they really are, and that kind of frustrates me. I like to talk about stuff, but a large chunk of the people here are into football and drinking beer. I like to have a good time, but there's more to life than that."

Loneliness has been a problem, Mike says. But he's been coping by forcing himself to remain social instead of retreating emotionally. "I've made myself keep going out there to meet people and not isolating myself. So I have started meeting a lot of people who I can talk to, but it's kind of frustrating. The people in the dorm, their priorities are just so different from mine. My roommate is the way I was three years ago. He and the guys in my dorm are not into expressing their feelings and any weakness is not accepted at all. They're into proving their masculinity and I don't think that's necessary. I'm comfortable with who I am, so I don't need to prove it to anyone."

Still, he admits that he has to struggle sometimes with his insecurities. "I have a fear of being alone. And so I've been kind of freaking out and going, 'Oh my God, there's no one here I can talk to.' So I write letters to people and I write a journal and I call my parents and talk to them and I have met some people here who I can be vulnerable with and tell them what's going on without them saying, 'Dude, you're a wimp.' "

To keep his head above water and not use drugs, one of the things Mike does is to give himself reassuring psychological strokes. "I wake up in the morning and I just keep telling myself, 'You're a nice guy. You should feel confident about yourself. You're likable.' "

Mike believes his insecurities can be traced to his parents' divorce. "My parents got divorced when I was eight years old. That was a real turbulent time. My mom [Sarah] was having a real difficult time, even before divorce, when I was six or seven. She kinda went wild for a couple of years. She was partying a lot, she had an affair with this guy, and then she left and went to Boston for a couple of years when I was seven. So she really wasn't there for me as a mother. And I had a lot of fear about being abandoned, because she left me and I had no mom. So that made me pretty insecure. . . . There was this point when one day I just woke up and I didn't like myself and I couldn't get rid of that feeling." He knows all this about his mother's past because she told him some years later. "We're like totally good friends now."

Mike didn't really like Eve when his father married her. "My real mom is really relaxed as far as authority and rules and stuff and she's just more like a friend to me. Eve was real strict about things. She is really authoritarian; she's kind of a dictator. It was a pretty drastic change. For eight years I had been able to do these things, then all of a sudden there's this strange woman telling me to cut my hair, what's appropriate and what's not appropriate. I really resented it." Nowadays, Mike gets along with Eve—with reservations: "She really irritates me sometimes. I think she has a big control issue. She has to get her way and that kind of frustrates me sometimes."

Mike says he still has not worked out all of the kinks in his relationship with his father. "We get along all right, but there's still some unresolved stuff. My dad's a perfectionist, so I've always felt that I was never good enough for him. I'll feel really good about myself and I'll feel like I'm doing great and then I'll come home and it's just like, 'Mike, go take out the garbage' from my dad. They [his parents] complimented me a lot at graduation and said they were really proud of me, but I don't know. When I lived at home I just didn't get the recognition . . . well, maybe I sort of did sometimes, but I don't know."

Mike admits that his father has changed a lot since he got involved with Spring Creek. In fact, his father tells him now that whatever Mike does with his life will make him happy if it makes Mike happy. After a bit, Mike is even willing to admit that perhaps some of the problem he has with his father may stem from voices from the past. "He doesn't have any expectations for me and stuff. And I know that logically, but I still hear the old voices."

"I get along with my real mom the best of all three of my parents," Mike says. "She had a lot of problems growing up, but ever since about two years ago she's been taking really, really good care of herself and this is like the happiest she's ever been in her life. So we really connect in terms of talking about stuff." Reaching this stage took some effort, Mike recounts. "I didn't see her for several years because there was too much tension. She didn't get along with my dad or Eve and they didn't like her and she had been gone for a couple of years, so I had not seen her. . . . I had some problems with her leaving, so we had a lot of stuff to work out, too." Mike and his mother started the process of sorting out their difficulties when one of the therapists at Spring Creek asked her to visit the school. "She was there for a couple of days, so we talked about our problems and, eventually, over the course of the two years I spent at Spring Creek things sort of smoothed out."

All in all, Mike feels like a great deal has "smoothed out" in his life, particularly since he feels he now has a handle on his own best self. "When I went to Spring Creek I found out who I really was; I really learned what I thought was important in life, what I wanted to do in life. I have this great desire to want to help people that have problems. I sort of took a look at the world and saw how unhappy people are and how bad people treat each other—there's just a lot of unfairness. So, it just seems to me that as long as we're going to live here we might as well get along."

POSTSCRIPT

"The difference between Mike and Frank, in terms of progress, was night and day," explains Gary Kent, Frank's counselor at Spring Creek Community. "The first contact that I had with Frank was with a young man who was very verbally compliant on the surface and in the presence of adults, though he became very angry when he couldn't get what he wanted." According to Kent, Frank had a history of psychiatric problems, including manic depression.

Kent viewed Frank as a very dependent person. "Frank would never do anything on his own. He needed people to direct him, to nurture him, to protect him. He would seek this typically in his relationships with women. While he was at Spring Creek he got involved with a co-dependent little gal who would take care of him." After some time at Spring Creek, however, Frank was beginning to try to take care of himself, but "his neediness was so overwhelming he could not succeed." Frank tried to establish some distance between himself and this girlfriend, for example, but his efforts to keep her away only lasted for about a week. Being alone, Kent says, "would create such an empty space, the pain would simply engulf him. There was a great deal of fear involved whenever he was feeling that he was by himself."

Frank was very pleasure oriented. "His mode of escape was to drink his pain away or engage in some type of sexual activity." One of the techniques Kent used to attempt to help Frank was to require him to engage in regularly scheduled self-reflection. He was to compile a daily journal and record what caused him to demonstrate poor impulse control. "He was moderately successful, but he didn't have the discipline to keep it up."

Kent estimates Frank's emotional age at about six or seven, though he possesses "some real fine intellectual capabilities to process information." Yet, the counselor notes, Frank is weak in linking up cause and effect. "We were also very suspicious of an attention-deficiency disorder." Kent believes that Frank ran away from Spring Creek because of his frustration in dealing over and over again with the same problems. "He felt helpless to change his behavior."

Eve was the primary enabler of Frank, Kent opines. She took the responsibility for Frank's behavior. As a result, Frank has had difficulty sorting out who he is, where he stops, and where other people begin. "In a way, if you look at Frank's activity over the past two months [running away from Spring Creek and moving from one relative's house to another], his behavior is an acting out of his anger that Eve is no longer willing to play that role. And Frank is really trying to say to her, 'Hey, I'm out here hung out to dry, by myself, and I'm scared.'"

Still, Kent adds, "As long as there's someone there to bail him out he will continue with dysfunctional behavior. The worst-case scenario for Frank is that he'll end up behind bars with a full-blown addiction. Right now what needs to happen is for Frank to really hit bottom to become painfully aware that there are some pretty big consequences for the choices he makes."

Are Eve and Mickey really helping Frank by barring him from their home since he ran away from Spring Creek? Will hitting bottom cause Frank to want to change his ways? Chapter Four, "Raising the Bottom, or Hanging Tough Phase Two," takes a look at such issues and more.

❧ *4* ❧

Raising the Bottom, or Hanging Tough Phase Two

My psyche has been tortured by images that friends recounted to me of how my sister fared once I decided to hang tough and she hit bottom. More than one person who saw her during the period immediately following her departure from my home reported that she roamed the streets in dirty clothes too small to cover a stomach that held a seven-month fetus. Even today I squirm when I think of what she experienced and what my role was in contributing to that experience.

Yet there is something good to be said about this time in my sister's life: She did find a drug treatment center and she did manage to stop using cocaine before her baby was born. What I have since learned is that most often a drug abuser has to hit bottom to want help and ask for it. The chemically dependent person will not face the problems caused by addiction until he's painted himself into such a tight corner that only two options remain: to take positive action to improve his situation or to give up on himself.

96

My sister, for example, was forced to sleep in shelters for the homeless because she had burned virtually all of her bridges to family and friends. She had to range the streets during the day because the shelters in Los Angeles insisted that the homeless population vacate the premises by a certain early-morning hour. She tells me now that she "saw it all" during that time and that what she saw and experienced was pretty horrible. But the squalidness of her circumstance, coupled with the fact that she was carrying another life inside her, finally caused her to dig deep and pull upon an inner resolve to survive. My sister reminisces:

> At some point I just looked around and saw that I had to change. I saw that my world was caving in on me, that I had to pull myself up and out of my situation. I thought a lot about my baby. And I cried a lot. For a while, I thought if the worst came to be, I might have to give my baby up for adoption. That's not something I wanted to do, but I knew that I had to start thinking about my child, I had to start thinking about what was the best thing for my child. I was scared, too. I thought about what the cocaine might be doing to my baby. I started praying that my baby would be healthy, that if I stopped using cocaine right now there would be no effect on my child. Well, I stopped using drugs and my prayers were answered. I have a really healthy, chubby baby boy—and I'm proud of that.

Hitting bottom happens differently for different people. But what cuts across all manner of adolescent drug abusers is this: A child in trouble will only reach out for help when she feels boxed in and believes that her options are limited to that of progress-or-perish. The same bottom line, however, can be attained when you, the parent, intervene and paint your child into a corner rather than waiting for her to do the same. When you hang tough you are drawing a line to protect yourself and your family members from the dysfunctional behavior of your chemically addicted child. When Eve and Mickey in Chapter Three's case study refused to allow 17-year-old Frank to return to their household, they were hanging tough by maintaining the integrity of their home and family. Once you refuse to enable your child and decide to look out for yourself instead, you have placed a mirror of sorts in front of your child. If you then provide your child with a way to receive help in a structured, therapeutic environment, you have engaged in a method of artificial intervention that's called raising the bottom, the second phase of hanging tough. Left to her own devices, your substance-abusing child can be expected to spiral downward in three stages.

THE DRUG-DEPENDENCY DOWNWARD SPIRAL

STAGE ONE:
IT'S JUST A PASSING PHASE

In the early stage of chemical dependency, the problems associated with the addiction are manageable. Your drug-abusing child doesn't feel she needs help. Moreover, if you, as a parent, are aware that your child is using drugs and the substances in question are gateway drugs—such as marijuana, beer, and cigarettes—which are considered the precursors to more hard-core substance abuse, you tend to feel no acute anxiety. Instead, you dismiss the problem. You tell yourself it will go away with time, your child is simply experimenting, doing what's natural to grow up. Some parents are so into denial during this phase that they don't even acknowledge strong indications that their child is using drugs—that she has become lethargic and her grades are beginning to slip, for example.

STAGE TWO:
THE MONSTER REARS ITS UGLY HEAD
AND DOESN'T GO AWAY

During the middle stage of a drug-dependency cycle, the drug problem is noticeable to others, although the child continues to deny that there is a problem. Now you are worried, though you may be at a loss as to what to do. Often, parents attempt to help during this stage in ways that really hurt the child. By providing the wrong type of support—making excuses, hiring lawyers, offering trips, nice cars, and nice clothes to their child as a bribe in hopes of making the addictive behavior go away—parents enable their children to continue to abuse drugs.

STAGE THREE:
HITTING BOTTOM

During late-stage dependency, the drug-abusing child is out of control. He can no longer deny that he is in trouble. He may run away from home because of his shame and fear of what he may do next. Generally, he has become part of a cadre of "friends" who are part of the local community's drug culture. This group lies, steals, and cheats others as well as themselves. At some point (as with Jeremy, the teenager in Chapter Two's case study, who finally stole from a neighbor and was incarcerated), the child will do something that boxes himself in so tight that he has no choice but to accept that he has hit rock bottom. When that happens, the child will commonly "relent and repent," according to drug-abuse experts, and either desperately seek help or readily succumb to parents' efforts to intervene. Tony, one of the young people interviewed for this book, is a real-life example of this downward spiral, of hitting bottom the hard way.

Tony was introduced to marijuana by his neighborhood "buddies" when he was only 14. It was not long before his school attendance and grades began to decline. Both parents knew he was using drugs but did not take the practice seriously. They became Tony's staunch defenders in discussions with school officials. By the time Tony was 17 and had graduated from high school, his drug habit had developed into both a cocaine- and alcohol-dependency problem.

Tony had no desire to continue school or to work for a living. His parents opted to let him stay home. He received what was equivalent to an allowance with no responsibilities attached and, in general, basked in the certainty of shelter and overall financial support. Every now and then, over a three-year period, Tony's father would find him a job, but Tony rarely lasted more than a month at such employment.

During this period, his chemical dependencies led him to start stealing valuable items from his home. When confronted by his parents, Tony lied. His mother tended to quietly accept her son's version of reality; his father would rant and rave but would not push Tony to produce the missing piece of property. Soon Tony began to get into trouble with the law. He was arrested several times for disorderly conduct such as fighting in a public setting, for possession of small amounts of cocaine, for driving under the influence of drugs and alcohol, and for other motor vehicle infractions. In each instance, Tony's parents came to his rescue by bailing him out of jail, securing an attorney, and welcoming him home with no demands that he change his behavior.

Finally, Tony's run-ins with the criminal justice system led to fines that were too expensive for his family to pay. Faced with a prison term and no parental rescue in the offing, Tony hit rock bottom and at that moment decided he needed help with his cocaine and alcohol problem. At 20 years of age, he signed himself into a residential drug-treatment center, in lieu of serving a two-year jail term.

What happened to Tony is common in terms of his downward spiral and in terms of how and why he sought help. Just like Aaron, the teenager who used and sold cocaine in Chapter One's case study, Tony managed to avoid going to prison by volunteering to be admitted to a live-in treatment center. When the criminal offense of a young drug abuser does not involve the use of weapons, judges have a tendency to be lenient if there is an effort on the part of the child to correct the drug problem.

The situation with your child does not have to reach such a low point. You can successfully intervene to thwart this process of downward projection.

ARTIFICIAL INTERVENTION: THE ROAD TO RECOVERY

The method of intervention called "raising the bottom" at drug recovery centers lets parents connect children, directly and painfully, with the consequences of their addictive behavior without endangering their lives. Often, for example, such children are isolated from their family and friends and made to live in residential treatment centers where their every move is monitored. Frequently, these facilities impose a strict regimen that may not even allow the child to make an unsupervised phone call. One of the first punishments Aaron, of Chapter One's case study, endured at a treatment center was for phoning a friend without permission. Jeremy, the teenager highlighted in Chapter Two's case study, made the point quite clearly that Spring Creek took control of his life in a way that he found displeasing, though now he seems to understand the value of such a tough method. Basically, then, when parents raise the bottom they artificially induce a late-stage crisis that causes substance-abusing children to feel as if their life has closed in on them.

A number of the parents I spoke to said the decision to take such harsh action against their child was a tough one to make, but most shudder to think of the consequences if they had not done so. The parents in this chapter's case study took a chance and intervened when their son was only 13 by enrolling him in a residential school many hundreds of miles from home. Though the final verdict is still out as to how Alex, now 14, will fare in the years to come, neither parent regrets the decision. In fact, what has since happened to their son's drug-using friends bears witness to the wisdom of the difficult choice these parents made. Alex declined to be interviewed for this book.

CASE STUDY:
ROBBIE, PETER, AND ALEX

Alex is an adopted child who was brought into Robbie and Peter's home when he was seven weeks old. He was 2½ when they divorced 12 years ago. According to 44-

year-old Robbie, however, "We were one of the first couples in the Santa Barbara [California] area to insist on establishing joint custody." Though Peter, 44, has remarried, he and his current wife live only minutes from Robbie—an arrangement that has allowed the ex-spouses to try almost "every permutation possible" with their joint custody agreement, in Robbie's words. When they first divorced, Alex spent three-and-a-half days a week with his mother and three-and-a-half days with his father. Then the schedule changed to one week at a time with each parent, then two weeks at a time. Finally, by the time Alex was 6, Robbie and Peter had settled on a formula that they felt worked: a one-month rotation at each home. "We went to one month so that everyone had the time to deal with issues and not be tempted to sweep their problems with Alex under the rug to deliver to the other parent," Robbie explains.

Alex has always known that he was adopted. Robbie and Peter told him all they knew about his birth parents. Alex has focused very little on the fact that he's adopted, so neither parent attributes his subsequent problems to that. Peter's current wife, Jodi, believes that Alex's behavioral problems stem from something else: "I think in Alex's early years both Robbie and Peter were very career oriented. I just think that he was hustled from one thing to another, from one parent to another."

Both Robbie and Peter are busy professionals. Robbie is a university professor who has earned two master's degrees; Peter runs his own real estate and property management company. Over the years, the two parents have also been involved in many community activities. In addition, Robbie has routinely sought additional teaching assignments and consultant work to finance vacations every summer for Alex and herself.

ROBBIE

Robbie recalls that Alex's problems first surfaced when he was in the fourth grade. "It was when the 'Night Stalker' was killing people [a murderer who was breaking into homes in Southern California late at night]. Alex was very, very concerned with this. He was concerned about people kidnapping him or breaking into the house. He was so afraid, he wouldn't even walk to the library." At this time, Alex asked to leave a mentally-gifted-minors program in which he had been enrolled for two years. The school counselor agreed that Alex could attend regular classes to relieve the pressure, and suggested that the parents seek therapy for the family and for Alex individually.

Robbie took Alex to see an art therapist, to whom he became greatly attached. The therapist died of cancer before she and Alex could have their last scheduled session. "Alex handled it very stoically, and I say stoically because it was as if Alex shut down," Robbie recalls. The next semester, during his sixth-grade year, Alex began to act out in class, giving his teacher some problems. By the time he entered the seventh grade, Robbie says, "In my mind all hell broke loose. He was growing very fast—he was obviously going through puberty. He started behaving as the class clown. He was experimenting with cigarettes. He looked as if he was using dope. It was as if the floodgates had opened."

From Alex's point of view, things were not as bad as they appeared to Robbie. "I'm just a teenager," he told her, "and this is what teenagers do." But, according to Robbie, all was not normal. Alex started getting lower grades—C's and D's, and an F in English, his former best subject. "He would do crazy stuff. He would do his homework but then leave it at home and not turn it in." However bad Robbie thought the seventh grade was, "The eighth grade was as if we were going downhill at a hundred miles per hour."

Alex starting hanging out with a group of five boys. They would hang up when Robbie answered the telephone. "I should have suspected something was wrong, but I didn't." Then Alex, who was 13 at the time, asked to spend the night at the house of one of these boys. Robbie agreed and met the friend's parent to make sure the arrangements were as Alex described. When Alex did not return on time the following day, Robbie called the friend's parent and discovered that the boys had spent the night elsewhere. "When he got home the next day I was hysterical and grounded him for one entire week. 'Lying doesn't cut it with me,' I told him." He behaved perfectly for the next week.

Then Robbie had to go out of town. She arranged for Alex to spend the time with his father, but Alex pleaded for another chance to sleep over at a friend's house, and eventually Robbie succumbed to his pleas. When Robbie returned home a few days later, she noticed that the quilt on her bed was not in the position she had left it. She also noted that some of her drinking glasses were not where they were supposed to be. "We've always had the agreement that kids aren't allowed in my house when I'm not home, so I cornered Alex and said, 'What went on in my house while I was gone?' Alex looked real nervous and denied everything." Robbie knew better than to believe his story.

She let him go to school without giving her a satisfactory answer. By the end of the day, she received a telephone call from the school informing her Alex had ditched all of his classes after 1:00 P.M. "I called Peter at work, had him pulled out of a meeting and told him he had to meet me at my house immediately. I ran to my next scheduled class and wrote a message on the blackboard that class was cancelled that evening."

When Robbie and Peter arrived at her home, they found a note from Alex that said, "I have to get away for a few days. I'll be okay. Please don't tell Dad." Alex had drawn hearts at the bottom of the note. All of his friends had left their parents similar letters, so all of the parents got together that evening to compare messages and to worry. One of the boys required insulin injections three times a day to control diabetes, so they called the sheriff out of concern for this child's life. After 24 hours, the boys called and asked to be rescued—they were 20 minutes away.

"They came back tired, cold, and dirty. We hugged each child and told him how much we loved him. Peter took Alex to his house, and we didn't let them go to school for one day. Since the whole school knew they had run away, we didn't want to encourage the return of the conquering hero." The next day one of the fathers confronted the boys with an accusation that the group had been using drugs. They did not deny the accusation. Alex became belligerent. He told Robbie that "nobody could tell him what to do." Alex's new and more intractable attitude persuaded Robbie that she could no longer handle him and that it was time to send him to some type of therapeutic boarding school. Robbie and Peter sought the advice of an educational consultant and decided on Spring Creek Community in Montana.

"It was the hardest thing that I've ever done in my life, sending Alex away. Peter and I cried and cried about having to do it." However, the chilling events that have transpired with Alex's cohorts since he was enrolled in Spring Creek have helped assuage any feelings she and Peter may have harbored that their decision was a mistake. Two of these 14-year-old boys, for instance, stole a truck and drove to Tijuana, where they were arrested and reported to the U.S. Border Patrol. All five adolescents were involved in a drinking and drug-taking spree that temporarily landed the group in juvenile hall and may cost their parents $400,000 because of a fire they started that burned down the administration office at their local high school. One of the boys was remanded to the California Youth Authority; one was sent to live in a group home; the diabetic child was placed in a drug rehabilitation center. "I feel as if I don't need to have any more data to let me know I made the right decision sending Alex away," Robbie concludes.

PETER

According to Peter, Alex's downfall began during his sixth-grade year when he went away to science camp for a week during spring vacation. "Alex came back a completely different person. It was as if somebody had turned the switch. He went away a kid and came back a young-man-in-the-making, and he was much less willing to take any direction from anyone." By the seventh grade, "Alex was just not fitting into the world in any way. I started thinking about sending him away, but Robbie wouldn't do it. Then Alex decided that he wanted to live with Robbie full time. At first I was hurt, but then I found out that it wasn't that he wanted to be with Robbie, it was that he wanted to be with his friends, who lived closer to Robbie than to my house."

Alex's behavior took an even sharper turn for the worse during the eighth grade. "As we tightened up and tightened up, he would do his homework but then he simply wouldn't turn it in. He also starting dressing like the

group of kids that you don't want your kid to dress like."
The final cataclysmic event, Peter remarks, took place
when Alex ran away. "Fortunately it rained and it was a
very cold night, so the kids returned the next day very
bedraggled.

"We learned, though, that Alex and his friends were
using marijuana, and we felt that this was not the way a
thirteen-year-old boy was supposed to behave." The next
step was to get Alex away from this environment. "We
arranged to have Alex spend a night at my house under the
guise that he was going to see his grandfather who had
come to visit for the weekend." The educational consultant
hired by Robbie and Peter handled the rest. "He woke Alex
up and informed him that he was going to be taken to
Spring Creek. Alex didn't try to get away once. In fact, he
almost looked relieved. Still, it was a difficult thing for me
to do, but I felt I had to do it."

Since he's been at Spring Creek, Peter says, Alex has
made "essentially no progress. He's decided the whole
world is wrong and he's right and that he's going to prove
it to the world. He told us he didn't want us to visit him
a few months ago, so we told him, 'If you don't want to see
us we won't come.' He's got to figure out who's going to
bend here, Alex or the world." Alex is also angry with
Peter because of the trouble Alex's group has gotten into
since he's been at Spring Creek. "His attitude was that if
he had been there this [the fire incident] wouldn't have
happened. Here he was looking at me straight in the eyes
and saying, 'I could have controlled the other boys.'"

No matter how Alex feels about things, Peter and Robbie have decided that he will remain at Spring Creek until
he's 18 or until he "figures out how things work in the real
world." But, Peter adds, "I miss him a whole lot and I think

about him a whole lot. I really wish he would figure out how the world works so that he's not unhappy the rest of his life."

POSTSCRIPT

"Alex is a very angry boy," reports Gary Kent, his counselor at Spring Creek. "He has a huge issue of being rejected by his birth mother. Alex still has to go through a real grieving about the loss of his birth parents and the divorce of Robbie and Peter." It's easy for Alex to be verbally abusive, explains Kent. But the counselor's diagnosis is that Alex's aggressive behavior belies a latent and deep-rooted insecurity. "Alex does a lot of pushing away of people on the theory that he should push them away before they push him away, as he perceives it."

Alex has been vacillating between compliance and defiance at Spring Creek. When he's in his compliance mode, Alex is trying to get released from Spring Creek, Kent notes. So far the tactic has not worked. "Alex will have to honestly confront some of his issues. Compliance alone won't get it." Not long ago, to move Alex along the continuum of cooperation at a little faster pace, Kent forced Alex to spend a period of time on the physical and social perimeter of the school because "that's the choice he has made when he chooses to be disinvolved." Alex's isolation involved being housed in a cabin outside of the main complex, though still on campus. He was also restricted as to who he might see or talk to. Alex was not allowed back into the school's mainstream until he was willing to genuinely participate in the treatment program. He lasted eight days in exile. Alex will be monitored regularly by Spring Creek staff, Kent says, to keep tabs on his sincerity.

"Alex is a very, very little kid, really, who wants to crawl into his mother's arms and receive nurturing. Robbie has a real desire and need to establish a close and intimate relationship with her son but doesn't know how to do this. She very much operates from an intellectual level." Kent believes that Robbie will have to take some real emotional risks to be the person she wants to be, and it's going to be a scary undertaking—especially, Kent says, "if you've been hurt."

Peter has been trying to rebuild bridges to Alex that they both have burned, but for the most part his son does not trust what his father is trying to do. "Peter, in his own words, feels that in his need to overcome his own handicap [a harelip] he's probably overlooked the needs of both Robbie and Alex." Regarding Alex's rejection of Peter, Kent adds, "I also think that Alex feels that if he reestablishes a relationship with his father, his father might go away again, he may just die or leave."

Robbie recognizes that her co-dependent behavior plays itself out in her tendency to withdraw emotionally in times of great conflict. "I call it taking a little vacation in my mind," Robbie explains. "I like to be a good girl. Still, I am controlling, but in a manner that is not direct and hostile. I control through organizing a person's day, his life. I organized Alex's notebooks for him, I restructured his schedule for him. I tried to make everything all better so that there was no verbal violence." This tactic put her at odds with Alex, who is verbally combative.

By intervening and raising the bottom of Alex's life, Robbie feels she has worked against her co-dependent habits: She set up a situation where Alex could stand on his own and learn to become his own person without her manipulations. So far, Alex has resisted efforts to counsel him at Spring Creek, but he has not tried to run away. Robbie has faith that Alex will come out okay at the other end of the process. "The environment of Spring Creek is an opportunity. It's teaching Alex that it's possible to respond to your emotional needs no matter the environment. There's always a boss and there's a price to pay, good or bad, for not playing by the rules. This action of sending Alex to Spring Creek was a very drastic step. But I feel that once you have done it, you have to see it through."

Did Robbie and Peter make the right decision to raise the bottom of their son's life before he did something that landed him in jail or that caused him physical harm? Or did they jump the gun? The tough decision that this couple faced to send their child to a residential treatment center will be explored in the following chapter, which examines the many treatment options parents have to choose from.

❧ 5 ❧

Treatment Options

My sister was seven months pregnant, lacking in family support and without funds when she went in search of a treatment program that would help her overcome her addiction to crack cocaine. Her options were limited, however, because of her pregnancy, financial status, and lack of insurance coverage. She did eventually enroll in a program, but some of the circumstances surrounding the experience worked against her recovery in several important ways.

First, not one of my sister's family members, including myself, was willing to take part in her drug therapy program. I was still of the opinion that my enabling behavior had been of some help to her—or, at least, should have been of some help. As I saw the situation, it was time for my sister to go it alone; I had gone as far as I was willing to go. In truth, my so-called help had been limited to providing financial support, since it was already late in the game when I was able to accept the fact that my sister's drug problem existed.

Likewise, my mother and stepfather took a distanced approach primarily because of their history with my sister. Every effort in the past to help her youngest daughter, my mother has oftentimes repeated, had caused family dissension and inevitably led to my sister's unceremonious departure from home or an ugly breach of some kind that fueled a temporary estrangement on the part of all involved. My mother said that she simply did not want to go through the pain of a familiar pattern. What my mother and I did not discuss, however, was that neither of us had ever really addressed my sister's drug problem. We had never attempted to steer her toward a rehabilitation program, and we had never taken it into account that we—my mother, my stepfather, or myself—could have been a part of the problem.

Although my sister was in her mid-twenties at the time, family involvement in her treatment program could have increased her chances for recovery, according to the National Federation of Parents for Drug-Free Youth. This organization reports that family participation in a young person's treatment program improves chances of recovery by ten times. In the absence of family involvement, explains California psychiatrist Loren Woodson, the only path of recovery is for the substance abuser to be able to say, "I want to save my own life." This is a tough road for a child to go down alone.

Getting help for your child, then, means that you should be open to securing help for yourself also. In fact, Steven W. Cawdrey of Spring Creek Community reports that the key to successful and speedy rehabilitation of the substance-abusing child is the extent to which the child's parents are willing to take part in the program and try to sort out how they themselves might grow and change. "At Spring Creek, parents are required to attend monthly parent groups. We even have a full-time family counselor. All that person does is call parents and ask, What are you doing in terms of getting therapy for yourself?"

Cawdrey adds that "If the parents can say, 'I'm really

tired of living this way' to themselves and mean it, if the parents can do this, the kids one hundred percent of the time see the parent as a role model, and the child's progress picks up almost immediately." In essence, raising the bottom for your child should mean that you are willing to raise it for yourself as well. No one said it would be easy, but taking the initiative to help your child and yourself is far superior to the alternative—continuing to deny and enable. Once you have reached this point of view and are ready to move forward to help your child and yourself, you will find various treatment options available, depending on a number of factors: your income level, geographic location, type of insurance coverage (if any), and ability to critically evaluate what is appropriate for you and your child's circumstances.

GETTING HELP

There are literally thousands of drug rehabilitation programs located throughout the United States, and hundreds based in Southern California. Yet my sister, roaming the streets of Los Angeles, had a hard time getting help once she was finally willing to seek it. Her problems were primarily threefold: She was pregnant, homeless, and virtually penniless.

Despite the alarming increase in the number of young, pregnant substance abusers, treatment programs dealing with this segment of the population are few and far between. Few programs are willing to take on the responsibility and potential liability of helping a pregnant woman withdraw from drug addiction.

My sister's homeless status also worked against her enrolling in an outpatient program. Participation in any drug treatment program requires discipline, which includes the willingness and ability to show up at the appointed hour on a regular basis. When you are one of the homeless, your precarious circumstances work against your reliability.

Also, since my sister was homeless, participation in an outpatient program would not have protected her from a drug-infested environment—an environment she would have no choice but to return to following every treatment session. Remember how the counselor in Chapter One's case study recommended that Aaron not return to his former environment upon completion of his long-term residential treatment, because it would be easy for him to reestablish his drug connections. My sister's homeless status posed the same threat in spades.

Moreover, her lack of money and insurance coverage worked against her enrolling in any treatment program, residential or outpatient. Treatment of a drug problem can become a very expensive undertaking. Low-cost or sliding-scale treatment centers are in short supply and thus have long waiting lists. The shortage of affordable treatment programs is especially critical when parents face what has become a relatively common judicial option: the choice for the substance-abusing child between a jail sentence and enrollment in a drug treatment facility.

Although close to 85 percent of Americans carry some sort of medical insurance, help in covering the expenses related to drug dependency is not widespread. As recently as 1986, according to a report issued by the National Association of State Alcohol and Drug Abuse Directors (NASADAD), only ten states required private insurers to cover alcohol- and drug-dependency treatment, and only two states required that purchasable policies be offered to cover the expenses of drug-dependency programs. Even

Medicaid, a program administered by states to serve low-income families who cannot afford medical care, does not universally provide coverage for drug treatment. (For a state-by-state list of health-insurance statutes as they relate to coverage for alcoholism and drug treatment services, turn to Appendix A at the back of this book.)

Although the current picture is somewhat discourageing, hope is on the horizon. Legislative measures in the public sector are moving in a direction that will improve health-care coverage nationwide for chemically dependent patients. A 1988 legislative update published by NASADAD shows that some significant changes have taken place:

> The District of Columbia, Hawaii, and Kansas now mandate insurance coverage for alcoholism, drug dependency, and mental health services.
>
> New York state now mandates coverage for outpatient drug-dependency treatment services, as well as for outpatient alcoholism treatment services.
>
> Pennsylvania now mandates coverage for alcoholism treatment services.
>
> Utah now requires insurers to offer, as an option for purchase, the provision of coverage for alcoholism treatment services.

According to documents prepared by NASADAD in 1988, new totals for the numbers of states that mandate coverage, require the offering of coverage for purchase, or have no relevant legislation are as follows:

> Twenty-five states and the District of Columbia mandate that private health insurers provide coverage for alcoholism treatment service benefits: Connecticut,

District of Columbia, Hawaii, Illinois, Kansas, Maine, Maryland, Massachusetts, Michigan, Minnesota, Mississippi, Missouri, Montana, Nevada, New Jersey, New York, North Dakota, Ohio, Oregon, Pennsylvania, Rhode Island, Texas, Vermont, Virginia, Washington, and Wisconsin.

Thirteen states and the District of Columbia mandate that private health insurers provide coverage for drug-dependency treatment service benefits: District of Columbia, Hawaii, Kansas, Maine, Michigan, Minnesota, Montana, Nevada, New York, North Dakota, Oregon, Rhode Island, Virginia, and Wisconsin.

Thirteen states require that private health insurers offer, as an option for purchase, coverage for alcoholism treatment service benefits: Alabama, California, Colorado, Florida, Kentucky, Louisiana, Nebraska, New Mexico, North Carolina, South Dakota, Tennessee, Utah, and West Virginia.

Eight states require that private health insurers offer, as an option for purchase, coverage for drug-dependency treatment service benefits: Alabama, Florida, Louisiana, Maryland, Missouri, North Carolina, Tennessee, and West Virginia.

Twelve states, as of January 1, 1988, had not yet passed any relevant legislation either mandating coverage or requiring the offering of coverage for purchase of alcoholism treatment service benefits: Alaska, Arizona, Arkansas, Delaware, Georgia, Idaho, Indiana, Iowa, New Hampshire, Oklahoma, South Carolina, and Wyoming.

Twenty-nine states have not yet passed any relevant legislation either mandating coverage or requiring the

offering of coverage for purchase of drug-dependency
treatment service benefits: Alaska, Arizona, Arkansas,
California, Colorado, Connecticut, Delaware, Georgia, Idaho, Illinois, Indiana, Iowa, Kentucky, Massachusetts, Mississippi, Nebraska, New Hampshire,
New Jersey, New Mexico, Ohio, Oklahoma, Pennsylvania, South Carolina, South Dakota, Texas, Utah,
Vermont, Washington, and Wyoming.

AVAILABLE TREATMENT PROGRAMS

Costs for the three basic types of treatment programs—
outpatient, residential, and long-term therapeutic care—
can range from as little as $100 for a one-time visit to
$25,000 or more annually. To assist you in seeking profes-
sional help for you and your child in all three treatment
categories, a list of drug-dependency centers throughout
the United States can be found in Appendix B at the end
of this book. Though the prices for such services can be
expected to change, the following represents a reasonable
estimate of costs as of 1988.

OUTPATIENT CARE

Typically, a four-to-six-week outpatient program can cost
$3,500 or much more, depending upon the particulars of
what is offered by the treatment center. Outpatient facilities can be found within hospitals and mental health clinics
or can be freestanding operations like those of Phoenix
House in New York and California. Outpatient care for
teenagers ordinarily requires that the youngsters come to
the clinic after school every weekday. You should expect to

be involved in the treatment program. Often, with outpatient care, therapy sessions are of two types: group meetings that include other drug abusers, and multifamily meetings where both parents and children confront, openly and directly, what is happening to the drug-dependent children and their families. Drug-abuse expert Steven W. Cawdrey describes it this way: "Our view of therapy is that both the parent and child must be put in the position where they are being challenged to calmly and constantly identify what they see in themselves that is healthy and unhealthy."

Outpatient treatment programs usually begin with an extensive one-time evaluation, which provides background information and determines the child's current drug-use status in order to fashion an individualized recovery program. An evaluation usually consists of information gathered from the parents; self-reporting during an interview with the child; reports from other counselors where a history of therapy exists; school records; police records and probation department evaluations; and observations of the counselor at hand. The following is an example of some of the information requested from parents on an actual evaluation document used by Spring Creek Community. Many programs nationwide require parents to fill out similar questionnaires.

> This information will be extremely helpful to us in constructing a clear picture of the applicant and the family dynamics. Please be as detailed as you feel necessary. Use additional paper if necessary.

> Name any significant family members or friends who are deceased. Please describe circumstances.

> Describe the following relationships in which applicant is or has been involved: each parent and/or

stepparent, sibling(s), and any other significant relationships.

Describe your relationship with your spouse, ex-spouse.

Specify any family member(s) who have in the past or are presently abusing/using or abstaining from drugs, alcohol, or nicotine.

Detail of family history in regards to alcoholism or drug addiction.

If applicable, describe applicant's adoption history.

Has the applicant been held back/skipped a grade in school?

If no longer attending school, give dates and details.

Describe any suspensions or expulsions.

Has the applicant ever used any of the following: Drugs? Alcohol? Nicotine? If yes, please specify and describe circumstances (i.e., substance, began at what age, behavior when using, etc.).

Has the applicant ever run away? Describe.

Tell us of any and all arrests, convictions, and probations; including age at time of occurrence.

Has applicant been involved in any physical, verbal, or sexual abuse situations that she or he initiated or was on the receiving end of? Please detail.

Describe your specific concerns regarding applicant's behavior, overall development, role models (adult or other), specific changes in behavior (dates, situations), pronounced changes in moods, eating habits, age-specific problems, and academic-specific problems.

Please list all professional treatment (hospital, treatment center, therapist, psychiatrist, etc.) applicant has utilized.

Describe any efforts made to resolve your concerns/ problems with applicant.

This particular therapeutic center also requires parents to sign a substance-test release, thereby allowing the treatment facility to administer, at random, tests to measure the patients' drug and alcohol use.

Such programs almost invariably include one-on-one counseling as well as family and group counseling. In group counseling, your child will be encouraged to talk about her history of drug use with other young people who have had similar experiences. The tone and tenor of the group often take a no-nonsense approach: Your child will be expected to own up to her problems. If she still denies that she is or was addicted to drugs, she can expect a tough and unyielding challenge by peers in the group and the counselor.

Spring Creek Community also works at developing self-esteem by requiring each student to complete two three-week courses called Survival and Challenger. As described in the school's literature, "the Survival course is a course like none other. Whether in the deserts of Arizona or the rocky crags of the Montana Rockies, students learn to survive using the same skills practiced by the ancient North American Indians." The skills demonstrated and taught include: Paiute bow-drill fire, shelter construction, water procurement, tracks and scat identification, edible wild plants, trapping with snares and deadfalls, and bow and arrow construction. The course covers 60 to 100 miles of varied terrain, with emphasis placed on individual achievement. The trips are led by certified survival instructors, male and female. Therapy is ongoing during the course and at weekly intervals in large groups facilitated by therapists.

Reports one teenager who had just completed the Survival course, "Three weeks ago I was certain I was a failure but now I feel I've accomplished a lot. I feel positive about myself and the way I look." According to Cawdrey, "This course helps those young people who need to discover and confirm their own capabilities as well as those children who are making a transition from a protective environment to one of choice and responsibility. . . . The Survival course is a form of artificial intervention, a form of raising the bottom. It's taking a tough stance with your child. It's creating situations for your child where realities must be faced."

The Survival course is a prerequisite for taking the Challenger course. Challenger is an adventure program designed to help students develop a healthy sense of interdependence, group communication, cooperation, and care for one another, as described in Spring Creek Community's promotional materials. The course is conducted in several of the high mountain ranges of Montana. The child is taught rock-climbing, backpacking, kayaking, cross-country skiing, snowshoeing, search and rescue, and canoeing, among other skills. Trust-building activities such as search-and-rescue and river crossings shift the focus from the individual to the group effort. Students are encouraged to reevaluate preconceived limits through activities such as rock-climbing and rappel (using ropes to descend cliffs). Through shared experiences in a physically and emotionally demanding environment, it is hoped that the children will come to realize that helping one another is the key to helping themselves. Parents are required to be present during the last four days of the Challenger course.

RESIDENTIAL CARE

The extra expenses associated with providing room and board, intensive counseling, and sometimes an educational curriculum are responsible for inpatient treatment costs of as much as $10,000 for a two-week stay. A candidate for residential care is typically a chronic substance abuser who has tried an outpatient program unsuccessfully. Given that scenario, parents and counselors tend to decide in favor of inpatient treatment programs when it is felt that a youngster needs to be removed from his environment. Again, the first procedure undertaken upon entering a residential facility is an extensive evaluation. If necessary, the youngster will embark upon a detoxification program, which can be gradual or cold turkey, depending upon the type of substance abuse, the child's health, and the policy of the treatment facility.

As with outpatient programs, the next step in the recovery program is usually individual, family, and group-therapy sessions to rebuild the child's self-esteem. For longer-term residential programs, nutritional education and planned physical activities are part of the overall treatment plan. Counselors also spend time with parents and the child in developing an aftercare plan to reduce the chance of relapse. Because the strains associated with returning to an unsheltered environment often become more than children or parents can handle by themselves, aftercare is a vital part of the recovery process.

LONG-TERM THERAPEUTIC CARE

If your child has been abusing drugs for a long time, you may have to consider a long-term treatment program, which can cost $30,000 or more per year. Montana's Spring

Creek Community, a 24-hour therapeutic boarding school designed for young people aged 13 to 18, offers programs that range from $7,000 for six weeks to $30,000 for one year. Treatment programs at facilities such as Spring Creek usually include a wide range of therapy modes.

Spring Creek emphasizes the development of emotional literacy skills. The students participate in eleven types of therapy applications that take up approximately 25 to 30 hours per week:

1. Individual therapy
2. Small group therapy, where the teenagers meet in groups composed of those who enrolled at Spring Creek at the same time
3. Large group therapy, where the entire teenage population focuses on a topic of concern to the therapeutic community. Prejudice against newly enrolled black and homosexual youngsters was one recent topic, for example.
4. Chemical dependency group therapy
5. Special boys' and girls' group therapy, where the children come together based on gender to explore issues of sexual identity
6. Leadership training group therapy
7. Immediate-response group therapy, which takes place when some type of disruption has occurred within the therapeutic community, such as a robbery, or when a child is in serious emotional pain
8. Family therapy/parent training
9. Individual crisis intervention
10. Recreation therapy

11. Daily living therapy, which takes place every morning and involves an evaluation of how the child is handling routine structure, chores, and interaction with the people he has to deal with in his daily living situation

In addition to the above therapeutic activities, children enrolled at Spring Creek Community attend classes from 9:00 A.M. to 3:00 P.M. and devote about 90 minutes per night to homework and preparation for the next school day. They are also required to engage in eight to ten hours of sports activities per week. "Our attempt is to create a model where there is an effort to teach balance," Cawdrey explains. "How do you take care of yourself on all fronts? Do you know how to ask for what you need?"

Even with the extensive counseling and schedule of activities, it typically takes a child approximately six to ten months to "move out of the honeymoon period and allow us to see the anger," Cawdrey says. "It takes about another eight months to a year before a kid finally sees the light." This schedule holds true most of the time no matter what treatment mode the child undertakes. Parents, Cawdrey adds, "typically take two years just to begin to unlearn the patterns of behavior they've acted out for so many years."

A positive as well as realistic interpretation of Cawdrey's prognosis is this: It has taken both you and your child a number of years to develop the problems that exist within your family unit; it will take some time to unravel what needs to be unraveled. But at least there is comfort in knowing that by seeking treatment for yourself and your child, you and your family members are spending your time wisely by building self-esteem and rebuilding fractured relationships, rather than acting out unhealthy behavioral patterns over and over again.

For the family in this chapter's case study, the willingness to try a number of treatment options for their daughter, Shana, over a three-year period has for the most part paid off. Shana is no longer using drugs; she is no longer acting out sexually; she has moved back into the home; and she is enrolled in school. However, an important problem this family faced—one you may have to face as well—has to do with the patience and persistence needed to identify treatment options that would best serve the family's particular dynamics and needs.

CASE STUDY:
LAEL, GEORGE, SHANA, AND SKYLER

Lael, 47, obtained her degree in social work from a major Ivy League college, but her experience in this field did not help her diagnose her daughter Shana's use of drugs, which began at age 15. "We were in a period of denial for a long time. We had no idea that Shana was involved with drugs and alcohol and [sexual] relationships," Lael explains. Her husband, 49-year-old George, has another explanation of why it took them so long to figure out what was going on: "Shana and I have always had an almost mystical relationship. We know what each other thinks. So she [Shana] kept up a pretty good face with me."

Lael and George have been married for 21 years. Lael, a director of planning and development for a nonprofit organization, prefers to describe her specialty as involving "the role of money in the public interest" rather than to be called a fund-raiser. George is an economic development advisor to the government of a country in Asia. They live in Washington, D.C., with Shana, who is now 17, and Skyler, 15. Both children were adopted.

LAEL

"When Shana was fifteen she ran away from home, and that just terrified us." Shana was gone for three days or so. Lael adds, "We didn't have any experience dealing with a runaway child. We were the family who all of the other kids in the neighborhood came to." From this point forward, the family "became a battleground of tremendous hostility against me after years of family togetherness. We went for a long time believing that this was just a normal period of adolescent obnoxiousness."

At first they thought a "good Quaker boarding school" was the answer, but then, "things went from bad to terrible." Shana attempted suicide, got caught shoplifting, and deliberately crashed her fist into a tree. Lael and George now know, but did not then, that Shana had started using drugs and alcohol in large quantities. "All the while, we were in therapy. Three and four days a week the family was seeing this top-notch therapist, yet we were being sucked into this vortex where nothing we did helped." Shana only lasted a couple of months at the Quaker school before the headmaster called Lael and George and told them to come get their daughter. School authorities felt that her emotional problems were too severe for them to handle. "Shana captivated people with her despairing behavior," Lael explains.

On Christmas day during Shana's fifteenth year, she told her parents that she had a drug and alcohol problem. "We were shocked. We were startled. For so long we had been telling our friends, 'We're sure Shana doesn't use drugs. There is absolutely no evidence that Shana is using drugs and alcohol.'"

During this period, George was approached by Harvard University to serve as a resident consultant, to advise the prime minister of an Asian country on international development issues. If he took the job he would have to spend a good deal of time away from home. Still, it was an opportunity of a lifetime. After some discussion, Lael says, he decided to accept the position.

"We had, up until this time, been living and breathing Shana, a child who had become a whirling dervish." The parents decided that the world "had to go on too." So George left for Asia and the family determined to start living its own life.

For a brief period, Shana appeared to be doing better. But then her behavior took a dramatic turn downward. She stopped going to school. She stayed in bed. "This was the first time she had done this. I was crying every morning on the way to work. 'I've done something to cause this,' I thought. 'I can make this child's life better,' I kept telling myself." Then on Shana's birthday, Lael found marijuana in her purse. The anti-depression medicine Shana's therapist was recommending could no longer be prescribed since she was using illicit drugs.

By this time, Lael winces to relate, "Shana was spending the night with boys, dressing like a mushroom in black, and sitting in her room that looked like a graffiti hellhole." Lael turned to educational psychologist Sidney Manning, who advised her she had three options: (1) Let Shana go out on the streets. (2) Write a contract with her daughter that outlined what Shana could and couldn't do, accompanied by agreed-upon sanctions. Given Shana's lack of resolve and discipline, Lael felt this option would be like "setting up an obstacle course for a paraplegic." (3) Establish an intervention process. Lael decided on the third option.

Meanwhile, Shana ran away to stay with a boyfriend but called after a few days to negotiate the terms of her return to the household. By then, Lael's brother had come to visit and to help while George was out of the country. "Shana actually had the nerve to call us and ask could she bring home this boy she had met who she wanted to come live with her at home. This kid was ten steps below Shana, but my brother and I pretended to go along with what Shana was saying, so she and the kid showed up at our door. Of course we grabbed Fu Manchu by the scruff of his neck and said, 'That's it, buddy,' and threw him out."

With the help of Manning, whom Lael refers to as Saint Sidney, it was decided that Shana would be placed in an adolescent drug treatment center called New Beginnings. "She almost seemed relieved when we told her there were no other options." To ensure that Shana did not run away again, Lael called upon some of the parents of a support group she was associated with to volunteer to guard the outside of Shana's bedroom door in two-hour shifts. Shana stayed put long enough to be escorted to New Beginnings a couple of days later.

Once enrolled at New Beginnings, Shana "was at first angry and into total denial. Then after a few weeks Shana called and said, 'Mom, I just want to be a normal teenager.'" Shana ended up graduating summa cum laude from the New Beginnings program after six weeks. Still, it was determined that Shana was not ready to return home, so Manning's advice was taken once again. This time, Shana was enrolled in Montana's Spring Creek Community. Shana accepted having to go to Spring Creek, her mother says, though she "groused a bit." She started by taking part in the school's three-week survival course wilderness experience. Immediately following Survival, Shana took the Challenger course.

In some ways it was harder for Lael to make the decision to send Shana to Spring Creek than it was for Shana to accept Lael's decision, because of the family's character.

"This is a very sort of democratically ruled family. We believe in consensus. Our democratic process, though, had to learn how to become very explicit and nonnegotiable." Six weeks after Shana entered Spring Creek, Lael saw her. "This kid had stopped smiling for a year or two. But when I first saw her after she had finished the Survival and Challenger courses, she looked great. Her eyes were bright. It was wonderful to see."

Shana stayed at Spring Creek from April 1987 to June 1988. During that period Lael visited the school four times. "I actually reached a point where I could look at Shana and say, 'You were so damn lucky to have me for a mother.'" Shana left the school because she wanted to attend her senior high school year in Washington, D.C. "We decided that there were some risks, but that they were well worth the risk." Shana is following an after-school care plan that includes therapy sessions with a psychiatrist, attending Alcoholics Anonymous meetings on a weekly basis, and participating in family activities.

GEORGE

"Shana has never been an easygoing person. She seems often to cut off her nose to spite her face. She exhibits a stubbornness that is difficult to deal with." Still, George adds, "We've had a special relationship, and she's held on to that through her darkest times." When she was 11 or 12, George says, Shana began to have annual blowups, cycles of explosions that usually took place around her birthday. "Shana had a tough adolescence. Among other things, she was raped."

As she progressed into adolescence, the signs that something was seriously wrong with Shana's life begin to pile up, but, George says, "We told everyone, 'At least

Shana doesn't drink, use drugs, or smoke. At least we know that she isn't doing that.' " Meanwhile, Shana had started running away from home. She changed her style to a punk look that included tattoos. When she was at home, she sat shriveled up in her room and had many sleepless nights. One time George caught her sleeping at 2:00 P.M. with her eyes dilated and barely able to lift her head, but still he told others, "Shana is not using drugs."

At the time, Shana was seeing a counselor who advised her against taking part in family therapy. George has some strong feelings about this counselor's competence. "There's so much bullshit surrounding the mental health profession. There's so much backbiting between the different schools of thought. We were shunted around in this whole mental health field—it was incredible. We knew our way around this profession, and as literate as we were, we were helpless throughout this period. At one point we had to just go in and say to the professionals, 'Now just a goddamn minute! We had to fight every step of the way."

Though Shana took her therapist's advice and resisted family counseling, she did indicate that she wanted to be removed from the home, where she did not feel safe from herself. The counselor suggested that Shana check into the Psychiatric Institute in Montgomery County, Maryland. The family complied, but, shortly thereafter, when the head of the Psychiatric Institute suggested family counseling, Shana "stonewalled because of the advice given her by her individual therapist," explains George.

Advice on what to do with Shana came from many fronts. "One schoolmaster said that the best thing we could do is just leave her [at his school]. Adopt the tough-love approach. Let her know that we meant business. When we enrolled her in that same school, she ran away within a day and turned herself in at the local police station. We picked her up and brought her back home on the basis of a contract we negotiated with her, a contract that committed her to go to school, participate with the family, and change her language.

"She did well that summer, so we enrolled her in another school . . . and thought the worst was over. But then she started using drugs and shoplifting. She was suspended and willfully did not abide by the rules. She was given a deadline to return the lipstick she had stolen to the store. She didn't return it. Our [Lael and George's] theory for why she didn't go along with such a simple request is that inside she knew she couldn't handle the drug scene. So she wanted to get out of that situation, but instead of dealing with the problem directly, she took the devious approach and got herself kicked out of the school."

George and Lael sent Shana to another school, but Shana soon ran away to move in with her "druggie boyfriend," George recalls. George was in Asia at the time. "I didn't feel badly that I was in Asia because we had done for years everything that we could do. It was time to let go and turn it over to someone else." That "someone else" eventually became the staff at Spring Creek Community, though Shana was first sent to New Beginnings to dry out. When she was released from New Beginnings, George received a call in Asia from Lael, who was terrified because Shana had reverted back to her "old stuff—sitting shriveled up in a corner."

But, as George later heard from Lael, "Lael and Shana got on a plane [to Spring Creek] and Shana went to sleep, and when Shana woke up she was a different person. Lael's firmness, Lael's clarity was a relief to Shana. Shana was determined to make her life work." While Shana was in Spring Creek, George talked to her regularly by telephone and visited her twice. "I had difficulties understanding and accepting the depth of Shana's problems." But during one of his visits, George felt that they became closer than they had been in years.

Shana's younger brother, Skyler, who accompanied his father, was not so impressed with Shana's progress. "Skyler is a very magnanimous fellow," George says. "He was understanding and thoughtful of Shana, almost too much and that was scary, but it seemed genuine. However, he was also angry and unforgiving."

Skyler demonstrated his frustration during this trip when he was asked to comment about his feelings. "I don't see any change [in Shana] at all; I don't feel one bit closer [to her]." When George tried to make excuses for Shana, Skyler followed up with yet another curt remark: "That's bullshit. She made the choices."

Essentially, George says, "Skyler saw what Shana's behavior had done to us and he hated what he saw. Skyler also probably guessed the price the family paid in purely monetary terms." (Because the family had minimal insurance, the final cost of Shana's treatment will be approximately $250,000.) Still, George confides that Skyler has handled the impact of his sister's drug abuse and related activities very well and has gotten over much of his resentment. Out of concern that Shana's problems could harm Skyler, George and Lael sent him to a therapist throughout the family's ordeal.

How did George and Lael's marriage fare under the stress of coping with Shana? "The common struggle did not bind us closer at first," George says. "Each of us wanted the other to solve it [Shana's problems with drugs]. Each of us tended to give lectures to the other, lectures that were really meant for ourselves. We blamed each other. We were used to being very compatible householders, yet during that period we were flailing around, grasping after theories of why this was happening, while phone calls from Shana's so-called friends interrupted our sleep in the middle of the night. We suffered tremendously."

Today, George says that his relationship with Lael has grown. "There's a richness for having experienced the vagaries of life . . . but it sure ain't fun," he adds with a quiet laugh.

SHANA

"At the end of the eighth grade, when I was thirteen, I was raped, and I covered it up for about a year," 17-year-old Shana says now in a matter-of-fact way. "The person who raped me was the brother of one of my good friends." Shana's parents had gone away for the weekend to do some white-river rafting, she recalls, and this guy rang her doorbell and "kind of pushed his way in, though he started off sort of friendly. I had been upstairs watching television, so I told him to come on up and watch the program with me. Once we got upstairs he raped me. I didn't want my parents to know that he had been over. I didn't want anyone to know what had happened. I felt scared and dirty, so I just kept my mouth shut."

Suppressing her feelings about the rape caused her to become depressed. Her grades started to drop, and "I started hanging out with a lot of hard-core skateboard punkers. I started getting into a lot of fights with my mom and dad. I was drinking occasionally, but nothing really bad—I just got drunk every now and then. I was fifteen years old and I wasn't using drugs yet."

Shana was dating a 15-year-old boy named Scott when she got into what she calls a "stupid big fight with my parents." Shana ran out of the house and Scott, accompanied by one of her friends, followed Shana to the Metro [subway] station. "Scott thought I was going to jump in front of a train, so he held me. I decided to run away and Scott said he wouldn't let me go alone." They caught a bus from Washington, D.C., to Myrtle Beach, South Carolina, and remained there for a couple of days. "Then we decided to go to Florida, so we started to hitchhike." However, before they could make it out of Myrtle Beach they were stopped by a man in his early twenties who invited them to stay with him.

"The place was horrible," Shana recalls. "Dogs urinated on the mattresses. The food was awful and there was another runaway kid who lived there. We couldn't stand it, so we rented a motel room." Then, Shana recounts, as they were walking around a shopping center, she fainted for lack of food. While she was being checked at a clinic, Scott was throwing up blood because he had a thyroid condition that had been aggravated by the harsh conditions they were living under. Eventually, Shana called her father and asked for help. George said he would have the police come pick them up; they ran instead. They only lasted a few hours, though, because of Scott's illness.

"When I went home I started seeing a shrink and was tricked into being placed at the Psychiatric Institute. I was pissed off for about a week, then I didn't want to leave." It was during this stay at the Psychiatric Institute that she mustered the strength to tell her parents she had been raped when she was 13. "When I told my parents, they were upset but acted kind of as if it was my fault. At least that's the vibes they were giving off to me. And at the time that I told them, I couldn't even say the fact that I was raped without breaking down and crying." Two months later when she was released from the Psychiatric Institute, things were so bad for her at home, she went to live with Scott.

Lael was a friend of Scott's mother, so she was able to live with this arrangement because the two mothers were working together, at least initially. "Scott's mom was like the mom I wanted," Shana says. "She talked to my mom, so it was okay that I stayed there." While living with Scott, Shana dyed her blond hair black and cut it Mohawk-style. "When I met my mother for dinner for the first time in a few weeks, my mom almost had a heart attack." Shana was sent to a school in Maine, but she ran away and went to a police station because she didn't have anyplace else to go. "So my dad came to pick me up, but I had to agree on a contract. The terms weren't harsh, although I thought at the time that they were harsh."

Shana spent the rest of that summer at the family's vacation home in Maine. During that period she started "getting drunk a lot, just to do it. I also started smoking marijuana." Her parents sent her to another boarding school, near Vassar. There she was introduced to marijuana that was laced with PCP and heroin. It was at this school that she attempted to commit suicide. "My new boyfriend cheated on me with my best girlfriend. When I found out I had a big fight with both of them." After the argument, she walked to a storefront area where the local teenagers hung out, seated herself in an alleyway, and swallowed "about forty Tylenol tablets with codeine." Another friend found her and took her to a teacher she was "close to." The teacher rushed her to a hospital, where she remained for a week. Both parents, she recalls, came and sat with her because someone had to be with her 24 hours a day.

Once she recuperated, Shana returned to the school, only to get caught shoplifting. "We would go on these binges to see how much we could steal, like lipsticks. I got kicked out for not returning the goods by the deadline that was set. I forgot [to return the stolen items] because it was around exam time and I was busy studying." Shana spent Thanksgiving of that year visiting a friend in Florida, where she got high and had sex without, for the first time, experiencing a flashback of the rape. "Then I thought, 'Oh, wow. I can have sex if I get high.' "

Shortly thereafter, Shana was enrolled in the Thorton Friends School in Silver Springs, Maryland. "Some of the student body used drugs like pot and drinking and took coke leaves." (Coke leaves, Shana explains, "are leaves of cocaine that you just chew up to make your mouth numb.") During her tenure at Thorton, Shana says, she also "did speed once." In the end, she was ditching school to get high and was suspended. Her parents got her reinstated at the school, but she kept skipping classes.

During January 1987, when Shana was about to turn 16, her father departed to go overseas. Shortly after he left she ran away with an old boyfriend, John. "My mom tricked me into coming home to sleep for a little while and then I was supposed to leave. Of course I was stupid enough to believe her. When I got there she got rid of my boyfriend and I was sent to New Beginnings. It is a forty-five-day program, but I stayed for sixty days. I was pissed off for the first two weeks, then I started to meet people and started to like it." Shana stayed in the program longer than usual because she had to make up for assignments she failed to complete during her initial period of rebellion. After completing the New Beginnings program, she was put on a plane to Spring Creek Community.

"I never liked Spring Creek. It was just another place where I was locked up. They control you." When asked how her stay there helped her, she answers, "I'm alive." She learned to appreciate the many therapy groups the school offers. "There's a lot of one-on-one therapy, there's group therapy, and there's family therapy. I dealt with my rape and my drug issue. I worked through a lot of stuff there during my first nine months."

Things went well for Shana when she came home from Spring Creek for Christmas vacation. She managed just as well during the following summer vacation with the family. At the end of the summer, a decision was made by her parents and the Spring Creek staff that Shana could return home.

Today Shana can identify what caused her to have such explosive fights with her parents, and she understands at least one reason she used drugs. "I've always been really impulsive, which was something I couldn't control. A lot of times the fight would be about me staying on the phone too long. If anyone said anything to me, I would get angry and walk off." She used drugs because "the flashbacks to the rape were not there when I was doing drugs. I did it [got high] so that I could sleep with boys and not think about the rape."

These insights and more have contributed to Shana's feeling good about herself. "I feel like I'm in control of myself now, like I know what I'm doing. It's just an overall feeling that I'm together and I'm me. When I go out and see drugs sometimes—and I do—I can't bring myself to use them. When I see people now who are drunk or stoned, I see how stupid they look." Shana reports that she has been completely sober one year and eight months and really enjoys how her life has changed. "I can play soccer and do physical things now; before I was too strung out. Now I can think straight."

She feels no bitterness now toward her parents for having "tricked" her at various stages in her recovery process. "I think my parents did absolutely remarkable considering what I did. If my mom hadn't put me in rehab and sent me to Spring Creek, I'd probably be dead right now. I'm happy that she did it." Shana is particularly pleased with what she learned about herself during the six weeks she spent in Spring Creek's Survival and Challenger courses.

"During the three-week Survival course you are starved for the first three days. You are in the Arizona desert and are allowed to carry a bare minimum of clothes wrapped in a poncho and blanket. You hike for about eighty-five miles during the course of three weeks. If you refuse to hike they drag you, they pull you along. People cut themselves to get out of it, but you don't get out of it, they just bandage you up and you have to still hike. You are taught how to make 'cold beds,' which is when you heat rocks and then dig up dirt to bury the rocks underneath to keep you warm.

"You make needles out of some type of animal bone. Finishing Survival makes you realize all of the things that you have. It makes you realize that life isn't so hard as you thought. I remember writing mom and saying, 'I'll eat anything you cook, just let me come home.' You also have a sense of accomplishment—you made it through this. It's like a one-day-at-a-time thing. I can't say that I'm glad that I did the Survival course, but to know that I made it through is good for my self-esteem."

Given her newfound strength, Shana offers a compassionate explanation as to why it took her parents a while to figure out what was going on with her: "My parents were naive at first. They believed that I wasn't using drugs. I hid it from them for a long time. They grew up in another era so they just didn't know. I'm grateful for them." Shana and her parents get along much better these days. "The way we communicate has grown a lot. My parents and I can talk about things now. And our fights don't escalate like they used to. When we get angry we just go away from each other.

"The only thing I'd like to know now is what my birth mother looks like. Until I get a good relationship going with my mom, I don't want to get into a thing of searching for my biological mom, and even then I just want to see what she looks like. A lot of people believe that an adopted child has to have problems with that [being adopted], and some do, but I don't."

Shana says she's trying to live by some of the values passed on to her by Lael. "She taught me to be my own person and she instilled in me that if you believe in something, [you should] stick with it, follow it, pursue it, and don't change your belief for someone else." Shana is currently in high school and attends meetings of Narcotics Anonymous and Alcoholics Anonymous. She plans to take a year off between high school and college. "I'm thinking now that I want to major in psychiatry. I would like to help others based on my past experience."

After Shana was raped, she says, "I didn't know what was going on. I was always down and upset. I even blacked out my childhood memories [from] before the rape. I forgot everything before that. Now I'm starting to figure out that I was a happy kid prior to the rape and that I'm happy now."

SKYLER

"In about the seventh grade I knew there were problems with Shana because she ran away on my birthday," explains 15-year-old Skyler. "I got really down when she didn't return. I stopped doing my schoolwork. I kept to myself a lot at that time. I was kind of distracted." On the other hand, all of the attention focused on Shana caused some resentment to well up in Skyler. "I felt ignored a lot. They [his parents] kept saying, 'Shana this, Shana that, will Shana ever turn around.' I got tired of dealing with it, hearing it, so I started moving on with my own life."

Skyler says he knew Shana was using drugs before his parents did, but he didn't say anything because "I didn't know how serious it could get." Why did he ignore her downward spiral? "I don't know. I didn't want to deal with it or her, so I just let it be." When his parents did find out about Shana's drug abuse, they asked Skyler to keep it a secret, but his friends already knew what was going on. "I've gotten into a couple of fights with guys who said something about Shana that I didn't like." He never told his parents or Shana about the fights, "because it's easy for me to hold things in." Lael tried to get him involved in Al-Anon (a branch of Alcoholics Anonymous for family members of alcoholics), but, he says, "I refused to go. I didn't think it was right for me. I didn't think I would get anything out of it." Skyler did go to family counseling, because "they made me go."

Skyler is not as confident of the solidness of Shana's recovery as is the rest of the family. "They think she's so-called cured. But it doesn't seem like a family to me. It seems like a movie, like somebody's writing lines for her to say. It's been a shock having her be good for a change. I think she's been busting her ass to be good, but Shana feels like a boarder to me. Half of me says, 'It's real,' but half of me says, 'Is it fake or is it real?' It's weird having her back home."

If Shana suffers a relapse, Skyler does not believe the family should invest any more money or time in her recovery. "The thing to say is put her back into treatment. But why put her through treatment again if she wants to mess her life up? It [more treatment] could change her, but I doubt it. It seems like a broken record to me for her to keep going through this [using drugs]."

Skyler's cynical assessment of Shana is tempered, however, by his final remarks: "I've always wanted to be close to Shana, to have someone to talk to besides my parents. I'm glad she's home. I'm going to work at being close, though I don't know how at this moment, but I'll just have to work that out along the way."

POSTSCRIPT

"I really grew up thinking that I could fix things and make people feel better. I spent lots of energy working the world around Shana," Lael explains. "I cannot say that we wanted to be victims, but we got locked into a kind of fear. We worried about Shana being out on the streets by herself. We worried about her use of drugs. There were times when we simply could not sleep because of the fear that some terrible thing might happen to Shana."

George echoes Lael's sentiments. "The three of us [Lael, Skyler, and George], at least, have determined that we are not going to live in that terror again. Shana's not going to live under this roof exacting the same toll. We can't make the difference if Shana doesn't want to live differently, but we are not going to live the way we did once before. We are concerned about family safety, and from now on we're going to take care of ourselves."

And, Lael is quick to point out, Shana will have to learn how to take care of herself. Lael believes, for example, that the "identity issue [dealing with the fact that Shana is adopted] is an important one for Shana, though she says it is not an issue." Now, however, instead of feeling that this is something Lael has to "fix," Lael believes the identity issue is something Shana has to cope with for herself. "I know now that that's a gap that she [Shana] has to fill."

Lael admits that some good things came out of her wrenching experience with Shana. "We're a much more explicit family now. We put the bad stuff right out on the table. I grew up not knowing how to express the angry stuff." Another plus: "My son and I got to know each other better." Indeed, she adds, "All of the members of the family are doing better as a result of this."

Have Lael, George, and Skyler reached the most healthy conclusions when they state that the family has gone through enough and now it is time to safeguard their own well-being? Are they being selfish or self-centered by drawing such a hard-and-fast line? If Shana is having trouble coping with her adoptive status, should she be left to her own devices to sort out any problems she may have with such a deeply emotional matter? You should already be able to answer the first two of these questions based upon what you've learned in Chapters Three and Four. You can find insight as to what might be an appropriate and healthy response to the last question in the final chapter, "Letting Go."

❧ *6* ❧

Letting Go

A close friend who felt she was doing a good deed brought my sister back into my life four months after she had delivered a healthy baby boy and seven months after she had unceremoniously exited my home. Up until that moment, I believed I had rid myself of my addiction to rescue my sister. I was confident I had my co-dependent behavior under control. I had faith that this time I had truly learned what it meant to let go and allow my sister to triumph over her own troublesome life.

It was the Christmas season, which is what prompted my friend to attempt a reconciliation between my sister and me. My friend called and asked if she could drop by since she was in the neighborhood. At the same time, she had picked up my sister, telling her that a mutual acquaintance wanted to see the baby. So we were both surprised to see each other. I wanted to hug her, but I would not let myself. I could tell she wanted to hug me, but she felt my reticence and refrained from reaching out. When she left I felt guilty and immediately began to devise ways to help my sister get on her feet, though I did not call it that.

At first I restricted my efforts to the baby. In my mind, it was okay to help my nephew because that would not count toward helping my sister; therefore, I would not be breaking my recently formed resolution to leave my sister alone. The memory was still fresh of how much money I had lost "helping" my sister, and I had not yet gotten over my resentment toward her for what I viewed as her abuse of my generosity.

On the other hand, I was afraid of what I might do once I saw my sister: I wasn't sure that I could trust myself to know just how far to go in terms of my new resolve. Perhaps what scared me even more was a nagging suspicion about myself: I wasn't sure I had the strength to stop myself from spending beyond a prudent limit. Why? In part I was unsure of myself because I felt guilty about having pressured my sister into leaving my home. Meeting with my sister to do some of the research for this book, I've come to an additional insight: I've also felt guilty about my sister's lot in life because I have been riding a tide of success that I didn't feel I deserved.

I was uncomfortable observing my very, very thin sister, who wore ill-fitting clothes, knowing that I had the money to upgrade her situation . . . especially after she told me she wasn't eating much in order to ensure that her cherubic-looking offspring ate as much as he desired. I accepted her explanation and started to purchase diapers and infant formula, believing that if I did this on a regular basis it would allow my sister to buy food for herself. There were a couple of critical circumstances, though, that I had chosen to ignore. First, I knew that my sister was living with the unemployed father of her child. Second, I knew that her boyfriend was using both alcohol and drugs.

My sister's weight did not pick up, even though my efforts to help did. In addition to buying diapers and formula, I offered my sister the job of transcriptionist and eventually paid her for services I never received. Finally, though, I exploded and decided, once again, that my role as helper simply had to cease. My sister was relieved because she saw my efforts as no more than patronage. She felt I had displayed a haughty pity for her rather than a genuine desire to help. Whether her assessment of me is correct I have yet to entirely sort out, but what I unequivocally gleaned from the experience is this: letting go is learning how to cope with chronic co-dependent and drug-dependent patterns of behavior. In essence, I supported my sister's relapse of sorts—her willingness to be rescued—and she supported my relapse—my anxiousness to be a rescuer.

These days, my sister and I have fashioned a very delicate relationship that entails keeping a respectful distance from each other. Occasionally we engage in long telephone conversations, but we rarely spend time together although she lives about a ten-minute drive from me. It is hard to break destructive patterns, but we are both finally ready to face that fact and rebuild our relationship carefully and with great caution.

SLOUCHING TOWARD RECOVERY

If there is a moral to be found in my personal experience, it is that letting go is an important part of the recovery process when dealing with a substance-abusing family member. It is also one of the more difficult parts of the recovery process to embrace, because it is often seen as abandonment rather than detachment with love. Parents who help their children overcome drugs are learning that they can only do so much; at some point parents must have faith in their child's ability to lead a productive life, although this may very well include periods of relapse.

Drug counselor Barbara Green of Pomona, California-based American Hospital explains why parents typically resist so strongly the concept of letting go: "Many times the need for a parent to let go is interpreted as indifference by the parent and by the child. It [letting go] brings out a lot of threatening issues, especially when dealing with a child. Parents are reinforced in so many ways for so many years that their role is to protect and to provide for the child. To detach, then, from their child is very hard for most parents."

Christy, Jeremy's mother in Chapter Two's case study, recounts how difficult it has been for her to let go and to accept her 17-year-old son's pattern of moving out over and over again to live with her ex-husband. "I've had to let go so many times, yet letting go has been a difficult thing for me to do. The first time I went through the process was when I made the decision to leave my husband, Richard. It was something I knew I had to do, so damn it, I was going to do it, but I didn't face what I was doing head-on. So it took years for me to really get over the experience.

"The next time I had to let go was the first time my son Jeremy decided he wanted to go live with his father. He was about eleven years old and I remember how he tried to help me let go by trying to talk with me, but I had a really hard time with it. It was really hard for me to let this happen gracefully. I just wasn't able to sit down with Jeremy and talk about what was happening. I don't think I helped Jeremy much during that move. When he left I sat down on the sofa and I drank a bottle of wine and I cried and cried and cried."

Currently, Jeremy lives with his father in another city. Jeremy calls her about once every couple of weeks and she writes him every week. Letting go is something she continues to struggle with, because "I still like to fix things, make things better for Jeremy, but now I can't do that, I just have to wait and see how it turns out for him."

Lael, the mother of Shana, 17, who provided testimony in Chapter Five's case study, says, "We're kind of letting go right now because Shana is in a lot of turmoil these days. We had a three-and-one-half month honeymoon with her [after her return from Spring Creek], and after a series of family gatherings she really crashed when her father left to return to his job in Asia. She's talking about wanting to leave home, but I think the turmoil is temporary. I think she's almost overwhelmed at her own success and she almost can't stand it. We've been bumping and grinding our way through this process for a while and what we've learned is that we can't coerce, force, fix, or change Shana. I can't make her happy."

Parents who help their children overcome drugs are learning that certain patterns of behavior displayed by both the co-dependent parent and drug-dependent child can work against the important step of letting go and can even lead to relapse for the entire family. This is so because of the interconnected symptoms of the parent and child. It is important that parents understand and recognize the three categories of warning signs that indicate the potential resumption of their co-dependent patterns of behavior, which can trigger a relapse of their recovering adolescent drug-abuser. The following lists are adapted from "Co-Alcoholic Relapse: Family Factors and Warning Signs," in *Co-Dependency: An Emerging Issue,* by Terence Gorski, president of Alcoholism Systems Associates in Hazel Crest, Illinois, and

Merlene Miller, director of education at Miller Intervention and Recovery Center, based in Olathe, Kansas.

EARLY WARNING SIGNALS

If you are experiencing five or more of these symptoms, there is reason to be concerned:

Situational loss of daily structure, such as a sudden inability to get to work on time

Lack of personal care

Inability to set and stick to limits with your children

Loss of constructive planning

Excessive or sudden pattern of indecision

Any type of sudden compulsive behavior

Fatigue or inability to rest

Return of unreasonable resentments

Return of tendency to control people, situations, things

Defensiveness

Self-pity

Overspending

Eating disorders—overeating or loss of appetite

Scapegoating

SIGNS OF A CO-DEPENDENT CRISIS

A co-dependent crisis is under way if you find yourself behaving in three or more of the following ways:

Sporadic attendance at formal support meetings or therapy sessions

Failure to maintain interpersonal (informal) support systems

Inability to construct a logical chain of thought

Confusion

Sleep disturbances

Behavioral loss of control

Uncontrollable mood swings

Feelings of loneliness or isolation

Emerging health problems

Use of medication or alcohol as a means to cope

THE DEBILITATION STAGE

You have reached the critical debilitation stage if you are experiencing three or more of the symptoms listed below:

An inability to change behaviors in spite of a conscious awareness that your actions are self-defeating

The development of an "I don't care" attitude

Complete loss of daily structure

Despair and suicidal thoughts

Major physical collapse

Major emotional collapse

LETTING GO WITH LOVE

The good news is that the worst-case scenario does not have to happen. Parents who help their children overcome drugs are learning how to detach from the symptoms of drug abuse exhibited by their offspring and to control their own symptoms of co-dependency. But, as Spring Creek's Steven Cawdrey points out, "Managing your symptoms is a forever program. You chip away at it a little every day. Since we are humans we are not perfect, so relapse on some level is inevitable."

Most treatment modalities in the area of drug abuse and co-dependency use, to some degree, the Twelve Steps of Alcoholics Anonymous as their practical underpinning. The Twelve Steps program is, in fact, a program geared to handling relapse. Letting go with love means that you understand that relapse is possible, perhaps even probable, but that you have enough faith in your child and in yourself to not rush to her rescue —one of your old patterns of co-dependent behavior. Letting go with love also means that you realize you deserve to protect and take care of yourself. To that end, you can reduce the risk of your own relapse and the risk of your child's relapse by taking on the following adapted list of doable tasks, developed by Gorski and Miller:

1. Become informed about what it means for your child to be addicted to her drug of choice. Understand the nature of the drug and what its impact is upon the user. Going to the library or bookstore to secure copies of books listed in Appendix C, "References and Suggested Reading," can help you become educated in these matters. Setting up an appointment to talk with your doctor is another way to get information. You can also obtain such guidance by calling one of the local drug treatment centers listed in Appendix B at the end of this book.

2. Become informed about the symptoms that accompany your child's recovery from chemical addiction. Whether you have opted to place your child in an outpatient or residential treatment program, the program's personnel should be able and willing to sit down with you and explain what to expect and help you handle the inevitable. In addition, the "References and Suggested Reading" list at the back of this book provides some basic explanations and descriptions.

3. Accept and recognize the symptoms of co-dependency—your reaction to a drug-dependent family member—by becoming involved in a support group like Al-Anon or your own individual therapy or family therapy through your participation in your child's treatment program, where you will be helped to develop a plan for your recovery. Addresses and telephone numbers for treatment centers as well as Alcoholics Anonymous, Cocaine Anonymous, Narcotics Anonymous, Drugs Anonymous, Al-Anon and Alateen, Drug-Anon, and Families Anonymous can be found in Appendix B.

4. Recognize the relapse potential of the adolescent drug abuser and of your own co-dependent behavior. Getting involved with support groups such as the ones listed above, where you share your own experiences and learn about the experiences of other parents and their substance-abusing children, will help you to accept the human condition which, by definition, means that none of us are perfect.

5. Develop a plan to prevent your own relapse, and support relapse prevention plans for your recovering drug-dependent child. "Self-discovery and growth requires consequences, not reactions," Spring Creek's Cawdrey explains. He suggests that you should develop a contract with and for yourself that ties you to consequences if any of the aforementioned symptoms of co-dependent relapse become apparent. For example, if you are a co-dependent person who falls easily into the practice of scapegoating, you could require that you make face-to-face apologies to the people you've blamed. Also, a good treatment program should have a strong aftercare component that includes preparation for relapse—yours and your child's.

6. Be patient with your own recovery and the recovery of your child. Neither of you became ill overnight, so recovery will take some time. However, be assured that recovery is possible. With effort, faith, and perseverance, dysfunctional families can be made whole, and committed parents can help their child overcome drugs.

The final case study for this chapter really encompasses all that the book has strived to make clear about how parents can, in fact, help their children overcome drugs. What I hope this case study demonstrates is what I hope the book itself has demonstrated: There is more than one definition of success and good familial health, and the key to such accomplishments has more to do with your and your child's willingness to work hard to change than with your and your child's ability to achieve perfection.

CASE STUDY:
MARY ELIZABETH AND PHILLIP

A New Yorker, Mary Elizabeth, 46, has been divorced for 13 years. She spent much of that time going back to school and getting a degree to develop her own career. Then she got so involved in the troubles of her son that there was no continuity in that career. Nineteen-year-old Phillip, she reports, has had difficulties ever since the divorce. By the time he started using drugs at 13, he had already been in therapy for six years.

Mary Elizabeth works from her apartment as a free-lancer coordinating special events in the arts. She has another son, Gregory, 16, who has just gone off to boarding school. She remains single. Her ex-husband also lives in New York City and has remarried, and his wife for a time tried to help Phillip during his struggles with drug abuse. On the other hand, Mary Elizabeth believes that her ex-husband has done some nonsupportive things that have actually hindered Phillip's recovery. Phillip declined to participate in this book project. Gregory agreed but could not be contacted at his boarding school in time to meet this book's press deadline.

MARY ELIZABETH

"The real problems with Phillip set in when he entered the eighth grade. He was thirteen and showing all of the symptoms of a kid who was experimenting with drugs and probably abusing drugs." These symptoms included: withdrawal; a change of friends to children who were equally withdrawn, sullen, and passive; loss of his former interest in athletics; erratic eating behavior, where he would be either ravenously hungry or not hungry at all; change in sleeping patterns so that he would stay up late and then sleep late and have trouble getting up; and "tuning out" in general.

"In the spring of his eighth grade I found some paraphernalia in his room, pipes for smoking marijuana and the paper that they use to roll the marijuana cigarettes," she remembers. Her response was to "address it for a very short time in the therapy that he was in. I brought up the fact that I had found it. I had allowed for about three weeks—once the issue came up about drugs—to see if any headway could be made. In the therapy I saw that there was no mileage being covered. Even though the information was out, Phillip was still resisting, there was still no dialogue. So I started looking into other alternatives in order to try to treat this problem."

There were programs in New York City specifically targeted to adolescents and drugs, and one was Phoenix House. Phoenix House had an outpatient program where children were required to attend group and family meetings every night but continued to go to school. "It's a very stringent, very demanding kind of program, and that's where I decided that Phillip was going to go. So I enrolled him in this program with a tremendous reluctance on his part, because he said he was using drugs so infrequently this was really an overkill to get him into a program for substance abusers. The doctor that was treating him also agreed [with Phillip]. He said that this was a drastic measure. I doggedly pursued it. There was a tremendous fear in me that if I didn't do something right now, he could slip into using even more drugs, and I wanted to confront the issue from the very beginning."

Mary Elizabeth now recognizes that her inclination to act and to act fast had as much to do with her co-dependency as it did with her fears of what might happen to Phillip. "I am a very confrontational person and also a very controlling person, so that this sort of satiated my hunger to keep it [Phillip's drug abuse] under control and pick up the baton and do something about it. There's something very, very assuring when there's a clear-cut action that you can take, there's a program that tells you what to do and that has a very clear-cut message. A lot of these drug rehab programs have a sort of zealot approach, which has its advantages and its disadvantages." The disadvantage, according to Mary Elizabeth, is that such programs leave you with the impression that there is only one way—their way—to pursue help. "This approach, of course, feeds into a lot of parents who are floundering and want someone to come in and say, 'This is the way to do it,' which prevents some type of assessment about what would be the most propitious route for each individual kid," she explains.

Phillip was substantially younger than most of the children in his group, who were juniors and seniors in high school while he was still in the eighth grade. Also, he was not as far along in his drug abuse as the young people he encountered at Phoenix House. Phillip remained in the Phoenix House program for over a year but did not "graduate," meaning he did not complete the program. "He did not respond to Phoenix House's group methods, and there was the tremendous disadvantage Phillip suffered under, which was that any program worth its salt requires the full participation on the part of the parents and I had an ex-husband who was very resistant. He was resistant to Phoenix to begin with, and he was resistant to the kind of demands that were being asked of all parents, which is essentially to question your own responsibilities and to risk opening up and sharing and exploring some painful issues that you might have with yourself or with your ex-spouse or with your child.

"My ex-husband was unwilling to try that out or to attempt to do that out of fear, out of anger." At one point, Phoenix House actually asked Phillip's father not to attend any of the family meetings, because he was not participating in a healthy manner and was demoralizing the rest of the group. He made fun of other parents and sarcastically questioned the leader of the group. Eventually, his word battles with the leader took up a lot of time in the group. "His attitude of mockery was very demoralizing for a lot of people who really wanted to work in the group," Mary Elizabeth says. "His attitude also derailed a lot of parents who were initially ambivalent and who found an ally in my ex-husband. . . . He is very resistant to any type of questioning of roles that should be played. For him that is hard to do and he was unable to do it. Since Phillip did not have the full support of both parents, it allowed him to play one off against the other and to manipulate, which drains all of the energy away from any kind of positive route that you can take."

Phillip simply did not respond to the method that Phoenix House employs. Later, Mary Elizabeth learned that some programs may succeed with some kids and fail with others. Phoenix House is very confrontational. "The idea was to try to tear down that brittle facade that the kids had built up for themselves. You had to be very forceful and very, very confrontational to tear it away. But with some kids, in the process of tearing it away, they [Phoenix House staff] did a lot of scarring, because these kids came in with some very fragile egos." Thus, she adds, "Depending upon the maturity of the kid who is going through this process, sometimes it worked to the child's disadvantage."

The technique worked for other children in Phillip's group, but not for him. "Phillip was almost like damaged goods when he left," she says.

"There is a process where you have to diminish and then grow. Phillip left the program prematurely because it wasn't working for him, but that meant he left before he could sort of grow up and put things back together again. If you fall apart and you don't have that other subsequent [rebuilding] process, it can be very damaging. I, being a distraught parent, stuck with the program too long, I think. And I think that the program at Phoenix House was too slow to acknowledge that perhaps Phillip needed another kind of treatment, because there are many different types of treatment and if one doesn't work there's always others." During the get-tough periods of his group sessions, "Phillip would withdraw and quite literally bury his head in his lap. And he never broke down. He just balled up into a tight ball. They were never able to get through to him by either having him break down, cry, or explode with anger—some type of reaction where he could open up and be a bit vulnerable."

Eventually, Phoenix House staff decided to allow Phillip a three-month probation on his own since he wasn't responding to their method and since he wanted so much to get out of the program. What troubles Mary Elizabeth now, though, is the fact that Phillip was not "clean," free from drugs, at the time he was put on probation. "They take urine tests, and they did not tell me at the time that Phillip was not clean. I had assumed that he was clean and that was why they were willing to take the risk of giving him a three-month probation period."

So Phillip left on those terms and, not surprisingly, was not successful. With the support systems that he had rejected at Phoenix House unavailable, he was completely on his own. "Despite the fact that he had resisted the program, there were friendships that he had developed among the kids and there were one or two counselors that had been there to support him, and then suddenly there was no program at all," Mary Elizabeth recalls. "So he did decline rather quickly during the summer of his ninth grade. I made a point of calling Phoenix House and making a special appointment to say, 'I feel abandoned; I need some guidance; help me.' Basically, they said, 'Let's just see what happens after the probation period.'" With that, Mary Elizabeth left the program bitter.

Phillip, then 15, developed a pattern that summer of running away and coming back. "He would just hang out with his friends. They would just take off. Phillip would only stay gone for about two weeks and he would always keep in contact with me, he would always have a note saying he was leaving. He was very confused, but he never lost contact with me. He would always make a call. His father over that summer did what he did from then on, which was to essentially write Phillip off when he was acting out. The message was: 'When you get your life together you can call me again.'"

When autumn arrived and the new school semester began, Mary Elizabeth wanted to adhere to the regular schedule she had been accustomed to, rather than tackling the more difficult issues surrounding Phillip's use of drugs. She fell back on "all of the little pegs that delineate your year, such as school starting in the fall." So she and Phillip "went through the procedure of trying to get into the routine of school, but it didn't last long—I think it lasted two days and Phillip was kicked out of school." He was asked to leave his prep school for violation of its strict dress code. The school required that Phillip's hair be cut a certain length and he decided not to comply. "So he went to school the next day and the headmaster called and said Phillip could not return until he got his hair cut. That was a real red flag, so the following day Phillip arrived with his hair uncut and was barred from attending class." To get Phillip under some kind of control, the headmaster suggested that Mary Elizabeth should threaten to send him to a public school; that, she recalls him saying, "should scare the shit out of him." "The public schools here in New York are quite different from public schools in other parts of the country," she says. "They're very tough. Walking into most of them could terrify anyone. It's predominantly minorities and it's large, impersonal, and sometimes frightening. There's a lot of violence in the public schools."

She ended up taking him to the best public school available in her neighborhood, and Phillip decided that he wanted to attend this school. Within the first month, however, he was pretending to leave for school but not attending classes. "In a public school setting, because of the number of students, the parents really are not notified about absences until about two months afterwards." Even before she was notified, she had noticed changes in Phillip. "He'd sleep late, then he would sort of drag himself out to school. Sometimes I would have to fight to get him out of the door so that he could try to get to school on time. His appearance became more and more disheveled. More calls were coming in [for Phillip] that were sort of odd calls from strange people with names that I was unfamiliar with, and that was a new wrinkle. In the past I usually knew the kids who called. I might not like them, but at least I knew them. In a private school setting you have class lists, you have parent meetings, so that names become familiar. But when you are dealing with a public school system, it's wide open, so you don't have a clue who these kids are."

During that year of Phillip's tenth grade, he plummeted. "By November, by the time I had gotten word from the school [that he wasn't attending], I knew that we were in deep trouble and I had already surmised that he was not going to school and had confronted him with my suspicions. . . . I was in such despair because I didn't have a Phoenix House to turn to for any kind of guidance. The psychiatrist I turned to was totally inadequate in terms of dealing with the whole drug issue." She ended up asking a priest for help and was told of a support group called Toughlove, made up of families in similar crises. She went to a meeting and found the support she was in search of.

"Toughlove was very helpful during the time that I needed it. It helps a parent begin to regain some type of control, and I mean control in the best sense of the word. Most of the parents, like myself, felt so out of control—not even knowing what to do either for the kid or for oneself. Many of the parents in this group who had been there a little bit longer really served as a support to try to regain some type of control over the situation and proceed in a way that would be not only healthy for them as parents, but healthy for the kids."

By the time Mary Elizabeth sought out the Toughlove group, Phillip no longer even went through the pretense of going to school. He just slept late, sat around the house during the day, and came in at all hours of the night. "I would lock him out and he would end up slumping on the outside of the door and in the morning there he would be. He was totally out of control. He was experimenting with all types of drugs. Anything that was available he tried, PCP, cocaine, heroin. Indiscriminately, he tried absolutely anything and everything that was provided for him.

"His mood swings would be very violent—either they were extremely low where he would be so despondent he wouldn't even be able to do the minimum of washing or eating, or his mood could be very violent, where his anger could be quite explosive and intimidating." She remembers how Phillip used to tyrannize both her and her younger son, Gregory. "He would go through the procedure of strangling his brother. Or he would scream and yell at me and push me up against the wall. He never hit me, but he was very intimidating in his whole manner. He would throw a dish down to the floor. He also stole money from the household. And every time I would impose even the most minor restriction he would fly into a rage."

Gregory survived this period, according to Mary Elizabeth, "by retreating into his own life. Once I saw him typing methodically, 'Gregory is great. Gregory is great. Gregory is great.'" Gregory found it difficult to openly share what he was feeling inside. "That concerned me," his mother says. Also, she adds, "When Phillip went to Spring Creek Gregory became very fearful. He wanted to be with me all of the time and he didn't respond to any type of therapy." As Gregory became interested in girls, he snapped out of it and concentrated more on his hairdryer, his mother reports, than on any trauma associated with or provoked by Phillip.

Meanwhile, with Toughlove, Mary Elizabeth got the support she needed to initiate a very dramatic action to control Phillip—to get a PINS (Persons in Need of Supervision) petition. In a PINS petition, parents give the court authority to control their child. In New York, this can be done before the child turns 16, when the child is considered a minor. "It's a very dramatic gesture. Most parents who do it are the poor and uneducated. They are the ones who usually resort to this procedure. I intentionally used it to see if there was a way of using it as a leverage to be able to regain control for myself as a parent. I was not doing it in order to relinquish my control or my responsibilities.

Basically, I was using it as a scare tactic to see if I could then get Phillip back into some sense of control, and I needed help on it."

To get a PINS petition, a parent must go to family court, formally request a petition, fill out the forms, and wait for the courts to request a hearing at which the child has to appear. The child is provided a court-appointed lawyer, and the parent can either hire his or her own attorney or do without legal representation. Then a formal hearing takes place where the judge determines what will be demanded of the child. Legally, the child must comply with whatever is demanded. The child's attorney is given the charge of protecting the child's interests, but that can mean many things. In this case, Mary Elizabeth's situation with Phillip was not really adversarial from her point of view. "I had a meeting with Phillip's lawyer so that he could see that we were both trying to do the same thing for him [Phillip]." She did not hire an attorney for herself. "I didn't feel like I really needed one, particularly since Phillip's lawyer concurred with me on the basic principles of what we were trying to do." The goal was to provide Phillip with some sense of an authority that he could listen to. In general, Mary Elizabeth wanted Phillip to be to frightened enough to want to do something to help himself. "The whole court procedure is very intimidating. It intimidates me, you can imagine what it does to a kid."

Phillip was not living at home when this process was taking place. "He was hanging out and spending the nights with people I didn't know." In court, a determination was made that Phillip had to go to a testing place called Geller House. Geller House is a state-funded, nationally renowned residential facility where children are assigned for six weeks to be tested and evaluated to decide where the court should place them. "That was the beginning of Phillip's feeling that there was someplace he could be that felt safe." However, it took a scare tactic to make Phillip consent to go to Geller House, since it is a voluntary program. "The other alternatives were that Phillip could either be sent home, because there's always that option if the parent will receive you, or be sent to a shelter. That was one of the most painful times that I had to make a decision, because at first Phillip said, 'I will not go to Geller House,' and I said I will not take my son back.

"The shelters in New York are very dangerous. You don't send a white boy into a shelter. The lawyer said so too. He said, 'Please don't send him there; he just won't get through. He'll either be abused physically or sexually.' But I said I would not take him. So when I left the court I left him behind knowing that he would stay in the courtroom until the end of the day, knowing that they would round up the kids, put him in a bus, and send him to a shelter."

Phillip bolted en route to the bus and got away. He was out on the street for two days, terrified, and then he called his mother and agreed to go to Geller House. At the end of the six weeks he went directly from Geller House to court. "The evaluation said that Phillip was not appropriate for what's called a therapeutic community. The therapeutic community, referred to by Geller House counselors, is a residential facility that is run by the state of New York for troubled adolescents who don't have substance-abuse problems. Phillip's evaluation stated that he needed a combination of a therapeutic community and some kind of drug rehabilitation." The report also indicated that Phillip needed counseling and psychiatric attention.

The therapeutic community didn't have the drug program that Phillip needed, though it did have the psychological support systems that were indicated. On the other hand, the local drug rehabilitation programs did not have a sufficient counseling and psychiatric function. So a compromise was struck: Since the Geller House counselors felt that Phillip needed to tackle his drug problems first, they suggested he be placed in a drug treatment center immediately, though they did not feel that was the ideal solution. An ideal solution would have been a drug program that had a very strong counseling and psychiatric component. However, Mary Elizabeth was told that the courts could not legally remand a child to a drug rehabilitation program because state funding for drug treatment programs had been severely cut a few years earlier. The courts could force Phillip into foster care through her PINS petition. "But foster care was not an alternative that would help Phillip, since that simply meant that he would be going from one family to another and not dealing with the issues. So I rejected that idea because I would only proceed if I knew that it would help him."

The court advised Mary Elizabeth that there was really nothing else the court could do for her. But, within the context of the family court, she was told that the judge could make it sound as if Phillip had to do what he was being told to do, although legally he did not have to comply. "We walked into the final hearing, Phillip had to stand up, and then the judge stood up to say, 'You have to do what your mother thinks is best for you.' Phillip bought that line. On the way out of the courtroom I told Phillip he had to go to the therapeutic boarding school I had found for him. Phillip did try running away, but I reminded him that the [PINS] process would start all over again, and this time he wouldn't be able to get away before he was delivered to a shelter." The threat worked. She got Phillip safely ensconced in the boarding school within 10 days of his being released by the courts. When she dropped him off, their farewell was amicable. "It was almost as if Phillip was relieved to be able to turn his life over to someone else, because I think he'd really gone through hell."

Phillip, then 16, ended up staying at the boarding school—Spring Creek—for two years. He resisted the school's program during his entire tenure, however. He ran away three times, the last time six weeks before his scheduled graduation. Whenever he ran away, Mary Elizabeth told him, "I will not receive any calls from you. Get back to school and we can continue this dialogue, but I will not talk to you while you are out on the streets." Though he did not return to the school to graduate, she says that Phillip did get a lot out of the school's program in terms of learning how to connect with people. "He began to start trusting some adults. He made some friends with counselors. He made some friends with his peers. He had some really good breakthroughs in terms of how he perceived himself, his relationship with me, and also his relationship with his father. When he left he was capable of setting some goals for himself that were more than 'I want to leave tomorrow; I want to get the hell out of here.'"

Phillip never completely accepted the school's program, his mother reports, but through the everyday experiences of living there for two years and having responsibilities that he either lived up to or not—and suffering the consequences of success or failure—he was able to begin to learn how to live in a safe environment. The last time Phillip ran away, he hitchhiked to Los Angeles from the Midwest, where he had some very bad experiences. "He was accosted by some homosexuals; he found himself penniless in the airport; he was very frightened. He was resourceful enough to find a family to take him in—a janitor who had watched him get attacked in the airport." After getting nowhere with his mother in his requests for financial support, Phillip managed to track down a nurse who had taken care of him when he was young, and she sent him the money for busfare home.

When he arrived home, Mary Elizabeth told him, "You can't come home until you can somehow prove to me that you want to do something for yourself. I'll put you up at the YMCA for two weeks so that you can at least be in a safe place, but you have to find a job and you have to find a support group." Phillip did both within the time frame allotted, and Mary Elizabeth let him move back. For one year, a lot of positive things happened. "Phillip was almost like the prodigal son. He returned and reestablished a close friendship with his brother. We began to learn again how to function, on a daily basis, like a family, which essentially we really hadn't been doing for more than six years. It was a lot of work for all of us, because we were sort of new at it, and it was successful in many areas. Phillip, as well as Gregory and myself, had really hungered for that kind of interaction. What a lot of families take for granted, like having dinner together where we all stayed until dessert, was a novelty for us. It felt new and different and reassuring and safe."

Phillip had a hard readjustment in terms of reentering into the general scheme of things outside the home. He was determined, though, to attend high school rather than test to obtain a General Education Diploma. Attending school every day and doing assignments were difficult for Phillip, but he persevered. He did not, however, respond to the therapy group he had chosen. "I had taken the stand that attending his group sessions was a requirement to stay in the house, but once again the scene repeated itself: Phillip went because he was told he had to go, so he went and just took up space. He didn't take advantage of the group."

In the spring of 1988, Mary Elizabeth reassessed Phillip's involvement in this group and came to the opinion that to continue was pointless; the group itself agreed. So Phillip stopped attending the group. He did graduate from high school and attended summer school because he wanted to get into Fordham University. But Mary Elizabeth started to see subtle changes in the way he cared for himself. "He began to have a harder time getting up in the morning. He was less motivated and just barely got through his summer school class.

"In looking back on it, whenever something has happened where Phillip was slipping and I had to get him back onto the right track, I have always used the same leverage: What does he want most? As a parent, how can I manipulate him so that I can have him do what I want him to do? In this particular case, as I could see that he was beginning to slip again, I did exactly the same thing. I said, 'Phillip, I know you're on drugs, I know you're slipping back into drugs, and I, as a parent, will not support that. I will not support, financially, your going to Fordham unless you can first acknowledge that you have a problem and that you're going to do something about it, so therefore college is out until you come to that realization. And if you don't, you're not even going to be able to stay in the house.'"

Phillip's response was to feel betrayal, anger, rage. "He said, 'How can you take this away from me? I want to go to college. Okay, so I've taken some drugs. I'll try to work on it. I slipped, but I'll try to do better.' But I said, 'That's not good enough. You get yourself into a program or you're out.'" Mother and son came to an impasse when Mary Elizabeth realized that emotionally she wasn't prepared to kick him out of the house; also, she began to examine how appropriate that action would be at this point. She started to wonder if his behavior really warranted such drastic action. "I began to question how effective this whole stance was, because I envisioned that if I succeeded again in forcing him into some other group, it would probably just be one more time that he went through the motions to stay at home."

Besides, she adds, "I was getting totally depleted and I knew that I had to examine what my responsibility was in terms of what I should do for myself and what I should do as a parent. And that's what started a whole sequence of perceptions about myself, that started tentatively and in a very confused manner, and in many respects I'm still very confused. But there was an incident that catapulted me into Al-Anon."

As the battle lines were drawn, with Mary Elizabeth on one side insisting that Phillip seek help or be kicked out of the house, and Phillip on the other side refusing to comply or leave, Mary Elizabeth remembers sitting on her bed and feeling a great deal of pain. "That pain was more than just the pain of a parent witnessing a kid floundering. I didn't know why it was more, but I just knew that it was. And it was so intense that I said I've got to examine this. Then I realized that a lot of that pain was that I realized that there was nothing more that I could do to fix it for Phillip. The phone was sitting in front of me, I remember, almost mocking me saying, 'There's no other program that you can call, there's no other therapist you can call. It has to, at some point, come from Phillip.' " Then I started going to Al-Anon, and the message there was very clear: The responsibility has to fall on the individual who has the problem. And there has to be a responsibility for yourself to start taking responsibility for your own life and your own attitudes."

Mary Elizabeth had spent virtually the last six years of her life so preoccupied with what Phillip was doing that she lost track of her own personal goals. "When I look at where I am right now, I feel depleted. And when I realized that there was nothing more I could do with Phillip, I couldn't fall back on any other thing that was nurturing because I hadn't created that for myself. So there was a tremendous loss and mourning that I couldn't somehow fill my life with some more solutions for Phillip. I also realized that I had hinged my own energy and moods to the success and failure of someone else, in this case Phillip, who basically I had very little control over."

To help her handle these painful insights, Mary Elizabeth started seeing the therapist who had worked with her to weather the storm of going through the PINS petition process of a few years before. This therapist's advice was: "You have to allow Phillip to try to sort out his own problems and to try to sort out his own mistakes. However, if Phillip is directly abusing you or destructive of something in the house, then you should address that kind of behavior, but otherwise you have to allow Phillip to take on some responsibilities."

As Mary Elizabeth has changed, she admits that there has been a small change in Phillip as well. "I'm allowing that to happen, though it's really hard for me to do. I have told him that I think he has a problem; that I hope he addresses it; he can make something of his life, but he has to make the decisions about how he wants to approach it. I suggested my therapist, however, he did make the call on his own; he has gone to her twice. And he said that he does want to go to college next semester. I said that he could but that he had to work between now and when school starts. Also, I told him that if he needed any guidance, here's a person you can call to help you sort out which colleges you want; he went to see that guy. He is looking for a job and it looks like he has one of his own choice, not one that I had suggested or through my contacts. And, finally, I'm backing off."

Phillip is still sleeping late, watching a great deal of television, remaining in isolation, and not seeing any of his friends, but that's his way of trying to stay off drugs, his mother reports. "That's short-lived, I know, but he has to find that out for himself, whereas before I would have said, 'That's not good enough. This is what you have to do and here are the programs, and you had better sign up with any of those programs within the next two weeks or you're out of the house.' I didn't do any of that this time. That's a big change for both of us."

POSTSCRIPT

All is not perfect for Phillip and Mary Elizabeth, but they appear to be off to a solid start in developing a relationship with each other, and with themselves, that is healthy and can be sustained over the long haul. The measure of their constructive teamwork, and how it has evolved for the better over the years, is best exemplified by Mary Elizabeth's newfound point of view: "When Phillip slipped there was a tremendous rage and anger that he had failed and that after all I had done for him, why wasn't he doing well? Basically, I had the power as a parent and I wanted to wield it while I had the opportunity, because the older they [children] get the less they need you. If I look at Phillip's and my relationship as two people rather than as a mother and child, I would never have treated him that way. The message for me now is, any type of recovery is a process. So you are going to slip, but then you get up and try again."

Mary Elizabeth has changed dramatically and so has her son. In the process she has, in fact, helped her child overcome drugs. She has also provided herself with the opportunity to live a full and productive life, albeit much work remains to be done for both her and Phillip to maintain their successes. Still, it's reassuring to know that what they have yet to accomplish in no way diminishes the quality of their current achievements.

What has provided the most inspiration for me, the author, in preparing this book has been the validation that recovery is the result of gradual but persistent attempts to change. Your willingness to persevere is something over which you do have control. That is an exciting concept because it's a goal that is within everyone's reach no matter how dark your days may appear at this moment.

Epilogue

Very few experiences take place in a vacuum. Writing this book was no exception to that rule. As I researched, interviewed, and wrote chapter after chapter, my own life moved forward in ways that influenced my approach to the preparation of this book. In turn, what I was learning about co-dependency definitely changed the way I handled my child and household.

My journey began when I decided to observe a multifamily group therapy session. It didn't take long before the leader of the group warned me that continuing with this project would not be easy. "You won't be able to escape your own stuff," he explained. I politely nodded that I understood and immediately adopted an attitude of mixed amusement and uncertainty. Thinking back, I realize that I didn't know what he meant, and I certainly had no idea of what would eventually come to pass.

"My own stuff" turned out to be my co-dependent patterns of behavior. Figuring out in specific terms what some of my "stuff" was, though, took time and was an evolutionary process of sorts. At that first family therapy session, for example, I thought that the participants' practice of starting each session with a greeting and an admission that they were co-dependents was a hokey thing to do. I simply saw no value in a person saying, "Hi, I'm a co-dependent and I feel pretty good today." Discussions about the concept of hanging tough seemed extreme to me as well. Yet, as I wrote the chapters and listened to parents and children tell me their stories, my attitude slowly changed.

Nowadays, I will quickly admit that I am a co-dependent person who has attempted to control my sister through my efforts to enable and rescue. It's important to me to have the courage to own up to what I am and what I've done. To that end, I've decided to share something I haven't shared until now: My co-dependency extended to my son also. For years I have felt guilty about not raising him in a traditional fashion. To put it simply (though still painfully), I never allowed my status as a mother to intefere with my professional ambitions. My son spent much of the first few years of his life with baby-sitters, for instance, because I was driven by a desire to obtain my college degree, and I did so without the benefit of family or spousal support since I had left my first husband when my son was in diapers and moved three thousand miles away from my parents.

So, as the years passed, I carried around a guilt that translated into a compulsion on my part to rescue my son whenever the going got rough, even as he entered his early twenties. I paid his parking tickets; I agreed to help him make his child support payments when, at age 21, he decided to quit his job and return to school though he had recently sired two children out of wedlock; I covered his long-distance telephone expenses (does this sound familiar?); and I told lies to protect him from the wrath of girlfriends who mistakenly believed in his fidelity.

It all came to a halt when I discovered that my VISA card, which I had allowed him to take to college, had been charged almost to its limit. I was nearing the end of this book when I learned this. By then, I had the courage to break my long-time pattern of co-dependency; having been exposed to the wisdom shared by the parents and children

I had interviewed, I understood why it was so important to hang tough and protect myself. Still, it was hard to take action and call the bank to cancel my son's credit card privileges. To make what I considered such a drastic move, I had to come to grips with my feelings about my relationship with my son, and my feelings about myself in terms of what I deserved in life.

To live fully, I learned from one of the counselors I interviewed, I had to learn how to deal with emotional pain. "After a while, you begin to understand," this counselor said, "that if you can handle the depths of pain you can also experience the heights of joy. . . . You can't shut down the bad stuff without also shutting down the good stuff." This dictum was made very clear to me when I met with my sister during the writing of this book and explored areas of sibling strife, resentment, and confusion that we had never before shared.

My sister pointed out to me, for example, that she was not the only child in the family to emerge with an addiction. Indeed, she reminded me, I had a history of compulsive spending. Somehow, I had managed to forget that I had at one time struggled mightily with this problem. As we continued our dialogue, I noted that I was afraid to ask her tough questions about the role I had played in her life. I was able, however, to silently question my fear, and I finally discovered what was really bothering me: I did not want to risk unearthing any additional evidence of my imperfection. My sister, on the other hand, seemed comfortable disclosing where she had fallen and where she had failed. I was shaken by her confidence and, at that moment, placed my co-dependent behavior under a brighter, more revealing light.

This experience allowed me to return to my manuscript with a more compassionate view of parents and their mistakes and why it is so hard for many mothers and fathers to move beyond denial toward recovery. My breakthrough with my son proved to me that this book was valuable, that what I had written could help others since I knew it had already helped me. What I hope, then, is that my story will help you step forward with faith and confidence to tackle the difficult process of recovery; in truth, by reading this book, you have already begun the process.

Appendix A
Summary of State Health-Insurance Statutes for Alcohol and Drug Treatment Programs

This list is derived from information provided by the National Association of State Alcohol and Drug Abuse Directors. It sums up the legislative requirements for coverage for alcoholism and drug-dependency treatment services on a state-by-state basis. If your state is not listed it means that, as of January 1988, your state had not passed any relevant legislation either mandating insurance coverage or requiring the offering of coverage for purchase of substance-abuse treatment benefits.

ALABAMA requires that alcoholism and drug-dependency coverage be offered by insurers and health maintenance organizations (HMOs).

CALIFORNIA requires that alcoholism coverage be offered by insurers.

COLORADO requires that alcoholism coverage be offered by insurers only.

CONNECTICUT mandates that inpatient treatment for alcoholism be provided by insurers and HMOs; also requires that outpatient alcoholism coverage be offered by insurers and HMOs.

DISTRICT OF COLUMBIA mandates coverage for alcoholism and drug-dependency services by insurers and HMOs.

FLORIDA requires that alcoholism and drug-dependency coverage be offered by insurers and HMOs.

HAWAII mandates coverage for alcoholism and drug-dependency services by insurers and HMOs.

ILLINOIS mandates coverage for alcoholism services by insurers only.

KANSAS mandates coverage for alcoholism and drug-dependency services by insurers only.

KENTUCKY requires that alcoholism services be offered by insurers and HMOs.

LOUISIANA requires that alcoholism and drug-dependency coverage be offered by insurers and HMOs.

MAINE mandates that alcoholism and drug-dependency coverage be provided by insurers and HMOs.

MARYLAND mandates that alcoholism coverage be provided by insurers and HMOs; also requires that drug-dependency coverage be offered by insurers.

MASSACHUSETTS mandates that alcoholism coverage be provided by insurers and HMOs.

MICHIGAN mandates that residential and outpatient alcoholism and intermediate drug-dependency coverage be provided by insurers and HMOs; also requires that coverage for inpatient alcoholism and drug-dependency programs be offered by insurers and HMOs.

MINNESOTA mandates that alcoholism and drug-dependency group coverage be provided by insurers and HMOs; also requires that alcoholism and drug-dependency individual coverage be offered by insurers only.

MISSISSIPPI mandates that alcoholism group coverage be provided by insurers only.

MISSOURI mandates that alcoholism coverage be provided by insurers and HMOs; also requires that drug-dependency coverage be offered by insurers and HMOs.

MONTANA mandates that alcoholism and drug-dependency coverage be provided by group insurers only.

NEBRASKA requires that alcoholism coverage be offered by insurers and HMOs.

NEVADA mandates that alcoholism and drug-dependency coverage be provided by insurers and HMOs.

NEW JERSEY mandates that alcoholism coverage be provided by group and individual insurers only.

NEW MEXICO requires that alcoholism coverage be offered by group insurers only.

NEW YORK mandates coverage for outpatient alcoholism and drug-dependency services by insurers and HMOs; also requires that inpatient alcoholism coverage be offered by group insurers and HMOs.

NORTH CAROLINA requires that alcoholism and drug-dependency coverage be offered by group insurers and HMOs.

NORTH DAKOTA mandates that alcoholism and drug-dependency coverage be provided by group insurers and HMOs.

OHIO mandates that alcoholism coverage be provided by group insurers only.

OREGON mandates that alcoholism and drug-dependency coverage be provided by group insurers only; also requires that alcoholism and drug-dependency coverage be offered by individual insurers only.

PENNSYLVANIA mandates that alcoholism coverage be provided by insurers and HMOs.

RHODE ISLAND mandates that alcoholism and drug-dependency coverage be provided by group insurers and HMOs.

SOUTH DAKOTA requires that alcoholism coverage be offered by insurers and HMOs.

TENNESSEE requires that alcoholism and drug-dependency coverage be offered by insurers and HMOs.

TEXAS mandates that alcoholism coverage be provided by insurers and HMOs.

UTAH requires that alcoholism coverage be offered by insurers only.

VERMONT mandates that alcoholism coverage be provided by insurers and HMOs.

VIRGINIA mandates that inpatient alcoholism and drug-dependency coverage be provided by group and individual insurers only; also requires that outpatient alcoholism and drug-dependent coverage be offered by group and individual insurers only.

WASHINGTON mandates that alcoholism coverage be provided by insurers and HMOs.

WEST VIRGINIA requires that alcoholism and drug dependency coverage be offered by group insurers only.

WISCONSIN mandates that alcoholism and drug-dependency coverage be provided by insurers and HMOs.

Appendix B
Resources

National Agencies and Self-Help Groups:

COCAINE HOTLINE
P.O. Box 100
332 Springfield Ave.
Summit, NJ 07901
(800) COC-AINE

NATIONAL INSTITUTE ON DRUG
    ABUSE
Drug-Referral Helpline
5600 Fishers Lane
Rockville, MD 20857
(800) 622-HELP

THERAPEUTIC COMMUNITIES OF
    AMERICA
54 West 40th Street
New York, NY 10018
(212) 354-6000

NATIONAL CLEARINGHOUSE FOR
    ALCOHOL AND DRUG
    INFORMATION
P.O. Box 2345
Rockville, MD 20852
(301) 468-2600

ALCOHOLICS ANONYMOUS WORLD
    SERVICES, INC.
P.O. Box 459
Grand Central Station
New York, NY 10163
(202) 686-1100

AL-ANON/ALATEEN
1372 Broadway
New York, NY 10018
(212) 302-7240

DRUG-ANON
P.O. Box 473
Ansonia Station
New York, NY 10023
(212) 874-0700

FAMILIES ANONYMOUS
P.O. Box 528
Van Nuys, CA 91408
(818) 989-7841

TOUGHLOVE
P.O. Box 1069
Doylestown, PA 18901
(215) 348-7090

NARCOTICS ANONYMOUS
P.O. Box 9999
Van Nuys, CA 91409
(818) 780-3951

The following is a partial list of treatment centers or extended care facilities that treat adolescents. Ages will vary.

ALABAMA

BIRMINGHAM
The University of Alabama
  at Birmingham
    Substance Abuse
    Programs
3015 Seventh Avenue South
Birmingham, AL 35233
(205) 934-2118

DECATUR
Charter Retreat Hospital
P.O. Box 1230
Decatur, AL 35602
(205) 350-1450

HUNTSVILLE
CareUnit Hospital Program
Humana Hospital
911 Big Cove Road
Huntsville, AL 53801
(205) 532-5222

ALASKA

ANCHORAGE
Charter North Hospital
2530 Debarr Road
Anchorage, AK 99514
(907) 258-7575

ARKANSAS

FAYETTEVILLE
Charter Vista Hospital
4253 Crossover Road
Fayetteville, AR 72702
(501) 521-5731

CALIFORNIA

ACTON
Acton Rehabilitation Center
P.O. Box 25
Acton, CA 93510
(805) 947-4191

AUBURN
Sierra Family Services
219 Maple Street
Auburn, CA 95603
(916) 885-0441

BELLFLOWER
CareUnit Hospital Program
Bellflower Doctors Hospital
9542 East Artesia
Bellflower, CA 90706
(213) 920-8826

CANOGA PARK
CareUnit Hospital Program
Humana Hospital West Hills
7300 Medical Center Drive
Canoga Park, CA 91307
(818) 712-4154

CORONA
Charter Oak Hospital
2005 Kellogg Street
Corona, CA 91719
(714) 735-2910

GARDENA
South Bay Chemical
    Dependency and Family
    Treatment Center

15519 Crenshaw Boulevard
Gardena, CA 90249
(213) 679-9031

GLENDALE
CareUnit Hospital Program
Glendale Memorial Hospital
    and Health Center
1420 South Central Avenue
Glendale, CA 91204
(818) 502-2361

HOLLYWOOD
Hollywood Community
    Recovery Center
1857 Taft Avenue
Hollywood, CA 90028
(213) 461-3161

INGLEWOOD
Inglewood Community
    Recovery
279 Beach Avenue
Inglewood, CA 90302
(213) 673-5750

LONG BEACH
Charter Hospital of Long
    Beach
6060 Paramount Boulevard
Long Beach, CA 90805
(213) 408-3100

LOS ANGELES
East L.A. Chemical
    Dependency and Family
    Treatment Center
3421 East Olympic Boulevard
Los Angeles, CA 90023
(213) 262-1786

El Sereno Chemical
    Dependency and Family
    Treatment Center

4837 Huntington Drive
    North
Los Angeles, CA 90032
(213) 221-1746

MOUNTAIN VIEW
Comadres
Family Service Association
655 Castro Street
Mountain View, CA 94041
(415) 968-3371

PALMDALE
CareUnit Hospital Program
Palmdale Hospital Medical
    Center
1212 East Avenue "S"
Palmdale, CA 93550
(805) 265-6410

PASADENA
Impact Drug and Alcohol
    Treatment Center
1680 North Fair Oaks Avenue
P.O. Box 93607
Pasadena, CA 91109
(213) 681-2575

POMONA
American Hospital
2180 West Valley Boulevard
Pomona, CA 91768
(714) 865-2336

ROSEVILLE
CareUnit Hospital Program
Roseville Community Hospital
333 Sunrise Boulevard
Roseville, CA 95661
(916) 781-1560

SAN BERNARDINO
CareUnit Hospital Program
San Bernardino Community
    Hospital

1500 West 17th Street
San Bernardino, CA 92411
(714) 887-8111

TARZANA
Tarzana Treatment Center
18646 Oxnard Street
Tarzana, CA 91356
(818) 996-1051

TORRANCE
Charter Pacific Hospital
4025 West 226th Street
Torrance, CA 90509
(213) 373-0261

VENICE
Phoenix House/Tuum Est
503 Ocean Front Walk
Venice, CA 90291
(213) 392-3070

COLORADO

AURORA
CareUnit of Colorado
1290 South Potomac
Aurora, CO 80012
(303) 745-2273

LAKEWOOD
Cenikor
1533 Glen Ayr Drive
Lakewood, CO 80215
(303) 234-1288

THORTON
CareUnit Hospital Program
Humana Hospital Mt. View
9191 Grant Street
Thorton, CO 80229
(303) 450-4500

CONNECTICUT

NEW HAVEN
Connecticut Mental Health
    Center
APT Foundation
Substance-Abuse Treatment
    Center
285 Orchard Street
New Haven, CT 06511
(203) 789-7387

NORWALK
Connecticut Renaissance
83 Wall Street
Norwalk, CT 06850
(203) 866-2541

STAMFORD
Liberation Clinic
125 Main Street
Stamford, CT 06901
(203) 324-7511

DISTRICT OF COLUMBIA

Second Genesis
1320 Harvard Street N.W.
Washington, DC 20009
(202) 234-6800

FLORIDA

CORAL SPRINGS
CareUnit of Coral Springs
3275 Northwest 99th Way
Coral Springs, FL 33065
(305) 753-5200

FORT LAUDERDALE
Spectrum
Financial East Building
2801 East Oakland Park
    Boulevard
Fort Lauderdale, FL 33306
(305) 564-2266

FORT MYERS
Charter Glade Hospital
3550 Colonial Boulevard
Fort Myers, FL 33912
(813) 939-0403

JACKSONVILLE BEACH
CareUnit of Jacksonville
1320 Roberts Drive
Jacksonville Beach, FL 32250
(904) 241-5133

MIAMI
Charter Hospital of Miami
11100 Northwest 27th Street
Miami, FL 33172
(305) 591-3230

New Horizons Community
    Mental Health Center
1469 Northwest 36th Street
Miami, FL 33142
(305) 635-0366

Spectrum
11055 Northeast 6th Avenue
Miami, FL 33162
(305) 754-1683

OCALA
Charter Springs Hospital
3130 Southwest 27th Avenue
P.O. Box 3338
Ocala, FL 32678
(994) 237-7293

ORLANDO
CareUnit of Orlando
1097 Sand Pond Road
Lake Mary, FL 32746
(800) 433-3691

ST. PETERSBURG
CareUnit Hospital Program
Saint Anthony's Hospital
1200 7th Street
St. Petersburg, FL 33705
(813) 825-1200

TAMPA
CareUnit of South
    Florida/Tampa
12220 Bruce B. Downs
    Boulevard
Tampa, FL 33612
(800) 367-3445

GEORGIA

ATHENS
Charter Winds Hospital
240 Mitchell Bridge Road
Athens, GA 30604
(404) 546-7277

ATLANTA
Charter Brook Hospital
3913 North Peachtree Road
Atlanta, GA 30341
(404) 457-8315

AUGUSTA
Charter Hospital of Augusta
3100 Perimeter Parkway
Augusta, GA 30909
(404) 868-6625

COLUMBUS
Turning Point
1220 Third Avenue
P.O. Box 2299
Columbus, GA 31993
(404) 323-3167

MACON
Charter Lake Hospital

3500 Riverside Drive
P.O. Box 7067
Macon, GA 31209
(912) 474-6200

MARIETTA
Straight
2221 Austrell Road
Marietta, GA 30060
(404) 434-8679

SAVANNAH
Charter Hospital of Savannah
1150 Cornell Avenue
Savannah, GA 31404
(912) 354-3911

IDAHO

NAMPA
CareUnit Hospital Program
Mercy Medical Center
1512 12th Avenue Road
Nampa, ID 83651
(208) 466-4531

ILLINOIS

AURORA
CareUnit Hospital Program
Copley Memorial Hospital
Lincoln and Weston Avenues
Aurora, IL 60505
(312) 859-0600

BELLEVILLE
Gateway Foundation
409 East Main Street
Belleville, IL 62220
(618) 234-9002

BELVEDERE
CareUnit Hospital Program

Highland Hospital
1625 South State Street
Belvedere, IL 61008
(815) 544-2273

CHICAGO
CareUnit Hospital Program
Mount Sinai Hospital Medical
Center
California Avenue at 15th
Street
Chicago, IL 60608
(312) 650-6509

CareUnit Hospital Program
St. Elizabeth's Hospital
1431 North Claremont
Avenue
Chicago, IL 60622
(312) 278-5015

EAST ST. LOUIS
Gateway Foundation
1509 King Drive
East St. Louis, IL 62205
(618) 397-9720

ROCKFORD
CareUnit Hospital Program
Swedish American Hospital
1400 Charles Street
Rockford, IL 61108
(815) 966-2273

SPRINGFIELD
Gateway Foundation
815 North 5th Street
Springfield, IL 62702
(217) 522-7732

WOOD RIVER
CareUnit Hospital Program

Wood River Township
   Hospital
Edwardsville Road
Wood River, IL 62095
(618) 254-0434

INDIANA

DYER
CareUnit Hospital Program
Our Lady of Mercy Hospital
U.S. Highway 30
Dyer, IN 46311
(219) 322-6802
(312) 895-9385

FORT WAYNE
CareUnit of Lutheran
   Hospital
3024 Fairfield Avenue
Fort Wayne, IN 46807
(219) 458-CARE

KANSAS

TOPEKA
C.F. Menninger Memorial
   Hospital Alcohol and
   Drug Abuse
   Recovery Program
P.O. Box 829
Topeka, KS 66601
(913) 273-7500

WICHITA
Charter Hospital of Wichita
8901 East Orme
Wichita, KS 67207
(316) 686-5000

KENTUCKY

ASHLAND
CareUnit Hospital Program
Our Lady of Bellefonte
   Hospital

St. Christopher Drive
Ashland, KY 41101
(606) 836-3148

FALMOUTH
CareUnit Hospital Program
Saint Luke Hospital
512 South Maple Avenue
Falmouth, KY 41040

LEXINGTON
Charter Ridge Hospital
3050 Rio Doso Drive
Lexington, KY 40509
(606) 269-2324

LOUISVILLE
Charter Hospital of
   Louisville
1405 Browns Lane
Louisville, KY 40207
(502) 896-0495

LOUISIANA

LAKE CHARLES
Charter Hospital of Lake
   Charles
4250 5th Avenue South
Lake Charles, LA 70605
(318) 474-6133

St. Patrick Hospital
524 South Ryan Street
Lake Charles, LA 70601
(318) 433-7872

NEW ORLEANS
Odyssey House Louisiana
1125 North Tonti Street
New Orleans, LA 70119
(504) 821-9211

SHREVEPORT
Charter Forest Hospital

9320 Linwood Avenue
Shreveport, LA 71108
(318) 688-3930

MARYLAND

ROCKVILLE
Second Genesis
14701 Avery Road
Rockville, MD 20853
(301) 424-8500

MASSACHUSETTS

BOSTON
Family Services Association
of Greater Boston
34 1/2 Beacon Street
Boston, MA 02108
(617) 523-6400

SPRINGFIELD
Marathon House
5 Madison Avenue
Springfield, MA 01105
(413) 733-2178

MICHIGAN

DETROIT
Family Services of Detroit
and Wayne County
Family Trouble Clinic
11000 West McNichols Road
Detroit, MI 48221
(313) 862-0330

GRAND RAPIDS
CareUnit of Grand Rapids
1931 Boston Southeast
Grand Rapids, MI 49506
(616) 243-CARE

PLYMOUTH
Straight

42320 Ann Arbor Road
Plymouth, MI 48170
(313) 453-2610

WEST BLOOMFIELD
Maplegrove Youth Treatment
Center
6773 West Maple Road
West Bloomfield, MI 48033
(313) 661-6507

MINNESOTA

MINNEAPOLIS
Fairview Deaconess
Adolescent Chemical
Dependency Program/
Riverside Medical
Center
1400 East 24th Street
Minneapolis, MN 55404
(612) 721-9722

Irene Whitney Center
for Recovery
4954 Upton Avenue South
Minneapolis, MN 55410
(612) 922-3825

MINNETONKA
Omegon, Inc.
2000 Hopkins Crossroads
Minnetonka, MN 55343
(612) 541-4738

PLYMOUTH
Anthony Louis Center
115 Forestview Lane
Plymouth, MN 55441
(612) 546-8008

Hazelden Pioneer House
11505 36th Avenue North
Plymouth, MN 55441
(800) 559-2022

ST. PAUL
Twin Town Treatment Center
1706 University Avenue
St. Paul, MN 55104
(612) 645-3661
(800) 645-3662

WAVERLY
New Beginnings at Waverly
Route 1 Box 86
Waverly, MN 55390
(612) 540-0005

WINNEBAGO
Winnebago Treatment Center
50 West Cleveland Avenue
Winnebago, MN 56098
(507) 893-4848

MISSISSIPPI

JACKSON
Charter Hospital of Jackson
East Lakeland Drive
P.O. Box 4297
Jackson, MS 39216
(601) 939-9030

MISSOURI

BRIDGETON
CareUnit Hospital Program
DePaul Health Center
12303 DePaul Drive
Bridgeton, MO 65044
(314) 344-7400

COLUMBIA
Charter Hospital of Columbia
200 Portland Street
Columbia, MO 65201
(314) 876-8000

KANSAS CITY
CareUnit Hospital Program

Baptist Medical Center
6601 Rockhill Road
Kansas City, MO 64131
(816) 276-7856

ROLLA
CareUnit Hospital Program
Phelps County Regional
     Medical Center
1000 West 10th Street
Rolla, MO 65401
(314) 341-2350

ST. LOUIS
CareUnit Hospital Program
Alexian Brothers Hospital
3933 South Broadway
St. Louis, MO 63118
(314) 772-4115

CareUnit Hospital of
     St. Louis
1755 South Grand Boulevard
St. Louis, MO 63104
(314) 771-0500

MONTANA

THOMPSON FALLS
Spring Creek Community
1342 Blue Slide Road
P.O. Box 429
Thompson Falls, MT
     59873-0429
(406) 827-4344
Program: Therapeutic
     boarding school

NEVADA

CareUnit Hospital of Nevada
5100 West Sahara
Las Vegas, NV 89102
(702) 362-8404

NEW HAMPSHIRE

DUBLIN
Marathon House
Box C
Dublin, NH 03444
(603) 563-8501

NEW JERSEY

NEWARK
Integrity House
103 Lincoln Park
P.O. Box 1806
Newark, NJ 07101
(210) 623-0600

PARAMUS
Fair Oaks Hospital
Outpatient Recovery Center
Bergen Medical Center
    Building
One West Ridgewood
    Avenue
Paramus, NJ 07652
(800) 872-3864

SUMMIT
Fair Oaks Hospital
19 Prospect Street
Summit, NJ 07901
(201) 522-7000

NEW MEXICO

ALBUQUERQUE
CareUnit Hospital
    of Albuquerque
700 High Street Northeast
Albuquerque, NM 87102
(505) 848-8088

NEW YORK

BRONX
Daytop Village
16 Westchester Square

Bronx, NY 10461
(212) 822-1217

BROOKLYN
Daytop Village
401 State Street
Brooklyn, NY 11202
(718) 625-1388

Phoenix House
55 Flatbush Avenue
Brooklyn, NY 11201
(718) 852-3150

JAMAICA
Daytop Village
166-10 91st Avenue
Jamaica, NY 11432
(718) 523-8288

LONG ISLAND CITY
Phoenix House
34-25 Vernon Boulevard
Long Island City, NY 11101
(718) 274-4213

NEW YORK CITY
Daytop Village
132 West 83rd Street
New York, NY 10024
(212) 354-6000

Odyssey House
309-11 East 6th Street
New York, NY 10003
(212) 477-9639

Phoenix House Riverside
    Center
164 West 74th Street
New York, NY 10023
(212) 595-5810

STATEN ISLAND
Daytop Village
1915 Forest Avenue
Staten Island, NY 10303
(718) 981-3136

NORTH CAROLINA

GREENSBORO
Charter Hills Hospital
700 Walter Reed Drive
Greensboro, NC 27403
(919) 852-4821

RALEIGH
Charter Northridge Hospital
400 Newton Road
Raleigh, NC 27615
(919) 847-0008

WINSTON-SALEM
Charter Mandala Hospital
3637 Old Vineyard Road
Winston-Salem, NC 27104
(919) 768-7710

OHIO

BARBERTON
CareUnit Hospital Program
Barberton Citizens Hospital
155 Fifth Street Northeast
Barberton, OH 44203
(216) 745-4114

CINCINNATI
CareUnit Hospital
of Cincinnati
3156 Glenmore Avenue
Cincinnati, OH 45211
(513) 481-8822

COLUMBUS
CareUnit Hospital Program

Mercy Hospital
1430 South High Street
Columbus, OH 43702
(216) 332-7348

Talbot Hall CareUnit
St. Anthony Hospital
1492 East Broad Street
Columbus, OH 43205
(614) 251-3760

DAYTON
CareUnit Hospital Program
Grandview Hospital and
    Medical Center
405 Grand Avenue
Dayton, OH 45405
(513) 226-3620
(513) 226-3312

MARIETTA
CareUnit Hospital Program
Marietta Memorial Hospital
Matthew and Ferguson Streets
Marietta, OH 45750
(614) 373-8816
(304) 428-2553

MILFORD
Straight
6074 Branch Hill
Guinea Pike
Milford, OH 45150
(513) 575-2673

MONTPELIER
CareUnit Hospital Program
Community Hospital
    of Williams County
909 Snyder Avenue
Montpelier, OH 43543
(419) 485-5511

OBERLIN
CareUnit Hospital Program

Allen Memorial Hospital
200 West Lorain Street
Oberlin, OH 44074
(216) 775-2273

SALEM
CareUnit Hospital Program
Salem Community Hospital
1995 East State Street
Salem, OH 44460
(216) 332-7348

WAUSEON
CareUnit Hospital Program
Fulton County Health Center
725 South Shoop Avenue
Wauseon, OH 43567
(419) 337-8661

OKLAHOMA

OKLAHOMA CITY
CareUnit Hospital Program
Saint Anthony Hospital
1000 North Lee Street
Oklahoma City, OK 73102

PENNSYLVANIA

ERIE
Abraxas II
348 West 8th Street
Erie, PA 16502
(814) 459-0618

HARRISBURG
Gaudenzia Concept 90
Harrisburg State Hospital
P.O. Box 10396
Harrisburg, PA 17105
(717) 232-3232

KINGSTON
CareUnit Hospital Program

Nesbitt Memorial Hospital
518 Wyoming Avenue
Kingston, PA 18704
(717) 283-2388

LIMA
Mirmont CareUnit
Mirmont Hospital
100 Yearsley Mill Road
Lima, PA 19037
(215) 562-9232

PHILADELPHIA
The Bridge
1912 Welsh Road
Philadelphia, PA 19115
(215) 969-8990

CareUnit Hospital Program
Osteopathic Medical Center
    of Philadelphia
4150 City Line Avenue
Philadelphia, PA 19131
(215) 581-6590

PITTSBURGH
Supervised Independent
    Living
241 Amber Street
Pittsburgh, PA 15206
(412) 441-5233

RHODE ISLAND

PROVIDENCE
Marathon House
131 Wayland Avenue
Providence, RI 02906
(401) 331-4250

SOUTH CAROLINA

WEST COLUMBIA
Charter Rivers Hospital
2900 Sunset Boulevard

P.O. Box 4116
West Columbia, SC 29171
(803) 796-9911

TENNESSEE

MEMPHIS
CareUnit Hospital Program
Saint Joseph Hospital
273 N. Parkway
Memphis, TN 38105
(901) 577-2902

TEXAS

AUSTIN
Charter Lane Hospital
8402 Crosspark Drive
Austin, TX 78761
(512) 837-1800

CANYON
CareUnit Hospital Program
Palo Duro Hospital
2 Hospital Drive
Canyon, TX 79015
(806) 655-7723

CORPUS CHRISTI
Charter Hospital of Corpus
    Christi
3126 Roddfield Road
Corpus Christi, TX 78414
(512) 993-8893

DALLAS
Help Is Possible
723 South Peak
Dallas, TX 75223
(214) 827-2870

FORT WORTH
CareUnit Hospital of Ft. Worth

1066 West Magnolia Avenue
Fort Worth, TX 76104
(817) 429-6763

HOUSTON
St. Joseph Hospital
1919 LaBranch
Houston, TX 77002
(713) 757-1000

LUBBOCK
Charter Plains Hospital
P.O. Box 10560
Lubbock, TX 79408
(806) 744-5505

MOUNT PLEASANT
CareUnit Hospital Program
Titus County Memorial
    Hospital
2001 North Jefferson
Mount Pleasant, TX 75455
(214) 572-1818

NACOGDOCHES
CareUnit Hospital Program
Memorial Hospital
1204 Mound Street
Nacogdoches, TX 75961
(409) 560-5200

SAN ANTONIO
Charter Real Hospital
8550 Huebner Road
San Antonio, TX 78240
(512) 699-8585

UTAH

MIDVALE
Charter Summit Hospital
175 West 7200 South
Midvale, UT 84047
(801) 561-8181

SALT LAKE CITY
Odyssey House of Utah
625 South 200 East
Salt Lake City, UT 84111
(801) 363-0203

VIRGINIA

ALEXANDRIA
Second Genesis
1001 King Street
Alexandria, VA 22314
(703) 548-0442

NEWPORT NEWS
Charter Colonial Institute
17579 Warwick Boulevard
Newport News, VA 23603
(804) 887-2611

RICHLANDS
CareUnit Hospital Program
Humana Hospital-Clinch
    Valley
2949 West Front Street
Richlands, VA 24641
(703) 964-9194

RICHMOND
Charter Westbrook Hospital
1500 Westbrook Avenue
Richmond, VA 23227
(804) 266-9671

WASHINGTON

ABERDEEN
CareUnit Hospital Program
Grays Harbor Community
    Hospital
1006 North "H" Street
Aberdeen, WA 98502
(206) 533-8500

ANACORTES
CareUnit Hospital Program
Island Hospital
1211 24th Street
Anacortes, WA 98221
(206) 293-3333

KIRKLAND
CareUnit Hospital
    of Kirkland
10322 Northeast 132nd Street
Kirkland, WA 98034
(206) 821-1122

SEATTLE
CareUnit Hospital Program
Ballard Community Hospital
5409 Barnes Northwest
Seattle, WA 98107
(206) 789-7209

CareUnit Hospital Program
Riverton Hospital
12844 Military Road South
Seattle, WA 98168
(206) 242-2260

SPOKANE
CareUnit at Garden Terrace
West 424 7th Avenue
Spokane, WA 99204
(509) 747-CARE

WEST VIRGINIA

WAVERLY
White Oak Village
Route 2
P.O. Box 56A
Waverly, WV 26184
(304) 679-3621

WISCONSIN

KENOSHA
Meridian House Ltd.
6755 14th Avenue
Kenosha, WI 53140
(414) 654-0638

WYOMING

CHEYENNE
Pathfinder
803 West 21st Street
P.O. Box 1604
Cheyenne, WY 82001
(307) 635-0256

Appendix C
Suggested Reading

Alcoholics Anonymous, Third Edition. New York: Alcoholics Anonymous World Service, 1976.

Donlan, Joan. *I Never Saw the Sun Rise*. Minneapolis: CompCare Publishers, 1977.

Grateful Members. *The Twelve Steps for Everyone*. Minneapolis: CompCare Publishers, 1990.

Hewett, Paul. *Straight Talk about Drugs*. Minneapolis: CompCare Publishers, 1990.

Kirsch, M. M. *57 Reasons Not to Do Drugs*. Minneapolis: CompCare Publishers, 1987.

Narcotics Anonymous. Van Nuys, California: Narcotics Anonymous World Service, 1984.

Nelson, Dennis, and Jane Thomas Noland. *Young Winners' Way*. A Twelve Step Guide For Teenagers. Minneapolis: CompCare Publishers, 1983.

Rosengren, John. *Young Winner's Guide to the Big Book*, For All Who Are Young and Recovering in Twelve Step Programs. Minneapolis: CompCare Publishers, 1990.

Schroeder, Bob. *Help Kids Say No to Drugs and Drinking*. Minneapolis: CompCare Publishers, 1987.

Index

About the Author

Born in West Philadelphia in 1950, Barbara Cottman Becnel still remembers how local gang members trampled freshly mowed grass and multicolored flower beds as they chased their rivals through the gardens of her middle class neighborhood. As a child, she watched and wondered about such sights; as an adult, she has devoted much of her professional life to developing public policy and programs that help children in trouble.

She has traveled throughout the United States and abroad giving lectures and conducting workshops about the complex factors that help perpetuate youth unemployment and crime; she also has provided testimony for Congressional committees in Washington, D.C., about these matters. With the writing of *Parents Who Help Their Children Overcome Drugs,* she has developed a set of guidelines for parents that will help prevent their children from becoming or remaining involved in the nation's drug culture.

Barbara Cottman Becnel moved to Los Angeles in 1980 from Washington, D.C., and has lived there ever since. Currently she spends her days employed as a consultant for the County of Los Angeles developing employment and training programs for the hardcore unemployed, including gang members, youth exoffenders, former drug users, teen parents, and high school dropouts. During the evenings (and sometimes early morning hours) she writes books. Her only child, a son, attends college in Sacramento.